DISCARD

Presented to
**Clear Lake City - County
Freeman Branch Library**

By

Friends of the Freeman Library

DISCARD

MYSTERIES, LEGENDS, AND UNEXPLAINED PHENOMENA

UFOS AND ALIENS

MYSTERIES, LEGENDS, AND UNEXPLAINED PHENOMENA

Astrology and Divination

ESP, Psychokinesis, and Psychics

Ghosts and Haunted Places

UFOs and Aliens

Werewolves

MYSTERIES, LEGENDS, AND UNEXPLAINED PHENOMENA

UFOS AND ALIENS

PRESTON DENNETT

Consulting Editor: Rosemary Ellen Guiley

CHELSEA HOUSE
PUBLISHERS

An imprint of Infobase Publishing

UFOS AND ALIENS

Chelsea House
An imprint of Infobase Publishing
132 West 31st Street
New York NY 10001

Library of Congress Cataloging-in-Publication Data
Dennett, Preston E., 1965-
  UFOs and aliens / Preston Dennett ; consulting editor, Rosemary Ellen Guiley.
    p. cm. — (Mysteries, legends, and unexplained phenomena)
  Includes bibliographical references and index.
  ISBN-13: 978-0-7910-9384-9
  ISBN-10: 0-7910-9384-0
  1. Unidentified flying objects—Sightings and encounters. 2. Human-alien encounters. I. Guiley, Rosemary Ellen. II. Title. III. Series.
  TL789.3.D463 2008
  001.942—dc22

                          2007029621

Chelsea House books are available at special discounts when purchased in bulk quantities for businesses, associations, institutions, or sales promotions. Please call our Special Sales Department in New York at (212) 967-8800 or (800) 322-8755.

You can find Chelsea House on the World Wide Web at http://www.chelseahouse.com

Text design by James Scotto-Lavino
Cover design by Ben Peterson

Printed in the United States of America

Bang EJB 10 9 8 7 6 5 4 3 2 1

This book is printed on acid-free paper.

All links and Web addresses were checked and verified to be correct at the time of publication. Because of the dynamic nature of the Web, some addresses and links may have changed since publication and may no longer be valid.

Contents

Foreword

Did you ever have an experience that turned your whole world upside down? Maybe you saw a ghost or a UFO. Perhaps you had an unusual, vivid dream that seemed real. Maybe you suddenly knew that a certain event was going to happen in the future. Or, perhaps you saw a creature or a being that did not fit the description of anything known in the natural world. At first you might have thought your imagination was playing tricks on you. Then, perhaps, you wondered about what you experienced and went looking for an explanation.

Every day and night people have experiences they can't explain. For many people these events are life changing. Their comfort zone of what they can accept as "real" is put to the test. It takes only one such experience for people to question the reality of the mysterious worlds that might exist beyond the one we live in. Perhaps you haven't encountered the unknown, but you have an intense curiosity about it. Either way, by picking up this book you've started an adventure to explore and learn more, and you've come to the right place! The book you hold has been written by a leading expert in the paranormal–someone who understands unusual experiences and who knows the answers to your questions.

As a seeker of knowledge, you have plenty of company. Mythology, folklore, and records of the past show that human beings have had paranormal experiences throughout history. Even prehistoric cave paintings and gravesites indicate that early humans had concepts of the supernatural and of an afterlife. Humans have always sought to understand paranormal experiences and to put them into a frame of reference that makes sense to us in our daily lives. Some of the greatest minds in history have grappled with questions about the paranormal. For example, Greek philosopher Plato pondered the nature of dreams and how we "travel" during them. Isaac Newton was interested in the esoteric study of alchemy, which has magical elements, and St. Thomas Aquinas explored the nature of angels and spirits. Philosopher William James joined organizations dedicated to psychical research, and even the inventor of the light bulb, Thomas Alva Edison, wanted to build a device that could talk to the dead. More recently physicists such as David Bohm, Stephen Hawking, William Tiller, and Michio Kaku have developed ideas that may help explain how and why paranormal phenomena happen, and neuroscience researchers like Michael Persinger have explored the nature of consciousness.

Exactly what is a paranormal experience or phenomenon? "Para" is derived from a Latin term for "beyond." So "paranormal" means "beyond normal," or things that do not fit what we experience through our five senses alone and which do not follow the laws we observe in nature and in science. Paranormal experiences and phenomena run the gamut from the awesome and marvelous, such as angels and miracles, to the downright terrifying, such as vampires and werewolves.

Paranormal experiences have been consistent throughout the ages, but explanations of them have changed as societies, cultures, and technologies have changed. For example, our ancestors were much closer to the invisible realms. In times when life was simpler, they saw, felt, and experienced other realities on a daily basis. When night fell, the darkness was thick and quiet, and it was easier to see unusual things, such as ghosts. They had no electricity to keep the night lit up. They had no media for constant communication and entertainment. Travel was difficult. They had more time to notice subtle things that were just beyond their ordinary senses. Few doubted their experiences. They accepted the invisible realms as an extension of ordinary life.

Today we have many distractions. We are constantly busy from the time we wake up until we go to bed. The world is full of light and noise 24 hours a day, seven days a week. We have television, the

Internet, computer games, and cell phones to keep us busy, busy, busy. We are ruled by technology and science. Yet, we still have paranormal experiences very similar to those of our ancestors. Because these occurrences do not fit neatly into science and technology, many people think they are illusions, and there are plenty of skeptics always ready to debunk the paranormal and reinforce that idea.

In roughly the past 100 years, though, some scientists have studied the paranormal and attempted to find scientific evidence for it. Psychic phenomena have proven difficult to observe and measure according to scientific standards. However, lack of scientific proof does not mean paranormal experiences do not happen. Courageous scientists are still looking for bridges between science and the supernatural.

My personal experiences are behind my lifelong study of the paranormal. Like many children I had invisible playmates when I was very young, and I saw strange lights in the yard and woods that I instinctively knew were the nature spirits who lived there. Children seem to be very open to paranormal phenomena, but their ability to have these experiences often fades away as they become more involved in the outside world, or, perhaps, as adults tell them not to believe in what they experience, that it's only in their imagination. Even when I was very young, I was puzzled that other people would tell me with great authority that I did not experience what I knew I did.

A major reason for my interest in the paranormal is precognitive dreaming experienced by members of my family. Precognition means "fore knowing," or knowing the future. My mother had a lot of psychic experiences, including dreams of future events. As a teen it seemed amazing to me that dreams could show us the future. I was determined to learn more about this and to have such dreams myself. I found books that explained extrasensory perception, the knowing of information beyond the five senses. I learned about dreams and experimented with them. I taught myself to visit distant places in my dreams and to notice details about them that I could later verify in the physical world. I learned how to send people telepathic messages in dreams and how to receive messages in dreams. Every night became an exciting adventure.

Those interests led me to other areas of the paranormal. Pretty soon I was engrossed in studying all kinds of topics. I learned different techniques for divination, including the Tarot. I learned how to meditate. I took courses to develop my own psychic skills, and I gave psychic readings to others. Everyone has at least some natural psychic ability and can improve it with attention and practice.

Next I turned my attention to the skies, to ufology, and what might be "out there" in space. I studied the lore of angels and fairies. I delved into the dark shadowy realm of demons and monsters. I learned the principles of real magic and spell casting. I undertook investigations of haunted places. I learned how to see auras and do energy healing. I even participated in some formal scientific laboratory experiments for telepathy.

My studies led me to have many kinds of experiences that have enriched my understanding of the paranormal. I cannot say that I can prove anything in scientific terms. It may be some time yet before science and the paranormal stop flirting with each other and really get together. Meanwhile, we can still learn a great deal from our personal experiences. At the very least, our paranormal experiences contribute to our inner wisdom. I encourage others to do the same as I do. Look first for natural explanations of strange phenomena. If natural explanations cannot be found or seem unlikely, consider paranormal explanations. Many paranormal experiences fall into a vague area, where although a natural cause might exist, we simply don't know what could explain them. In that case I tell people to trust their intuition that they had a paranormal experience. Sometimes the explanation makes itself known later on.

I have concluded from my studies and experiences that invisible dimensions are layered upon our world, and that many paranormal experiences occur when there are openings between worlds. The doorways often open at unexpected times. You take a trip, visit a haunted place, or have a strange dream–and suddenly reality shifts. You get a glimpse behind the curtain that separates the ordinary from the extraordinary.

The books in this series will introduce you to these exciting and mysterious subjects. You'll learn many things that will astonish you. You'll be given lots of tips for how to explore the paranormal on your own. Paranormal investigation is a popular field, and you don't have to be a scientist or a full-time researcher to explore it. There are many things you can do in your free time. The knowledge you gain from these books will help prepare you for any unusual and unexpected experiences.

As you go deeper into your study of the paranormal, you may come up with new ideas for explanations. That's one of the appealing aspects of paranormal investigation–there is always room for bold ideas. So, keep an open and curious mind, and think big. Mysterious worlds are waiting for you!

—Rosemary Ellen Guiley

Introduction

$\mathscr{E}$ach year, thousands of people report seeing strange, unidentified flying objects, or UFOs, in the sky. Some people also claim to have seen the **UFO** occupants or even that they themselves have been taken onboard! Unidentified flying objects have puzzled humanity for thousands of years. What are these strange objects in the sky? Where do they come from and why are they here?

The fact is, UFOs are seen all across the planet, on every one of the seven continents, in hundreds of different countries, and even over the oceans. They have been observed by all kinds of people from all walks of life, including police officers, pilots, scientists, astronauts—even President Jimmy Carter reported seeing a UFO! They come in many different shapes, sizes, and colors. They can move at great speeds or hover perfectly still in the sky. They have been reported for centuries and continue to be reported today. There are now several thousand reports on record, yet nobody knows for sure exactly what UFOs are.

To be scientific, it's necessary to take an objective look at the evidence. The question is not: "Are UFOs real?" People are definitely seeing *something*. The question is: "What exactly are they seeing?"

This book will explore the fascinating history of the UFO phenomenon, dating from ancient times to the present day. This journey through time will visit the various cultures of the world as they encounter UFOs for the first time. It begins with the Egyptians and Romans who encountered UFOs thousands of years ago, and then moves on to Medieval and Renaissance encounters, followed by sightings in the 1800s, the incredible airship wave of 1897, the "**foo fighters**" of

World War II, and the beginning of the Modern Age of UFOs starting in 1947.

Many of the world's best-verified and most exciting cases are covered in detail, as are the scenes of the world's most intense UFO waves, where strange objects hovered over people's homes, chased cars down highways, and performed incredible maneuvers in the sky. This book also examines the most famous UFO landing cases and describes instances when aliens exited their spacecraft to confront surprised humans.

The 1960s brought the first cases of UFO abductions and onboard experiences. This book will describe face-to-face encounters with extraterrestrials and explore what it's (reportedly) like to be taken onboard a **flying saucer** and meet with what appears to be extraterrestrials from other planets.

Today, the UFO phenomenon has become even more complicated with claims of UFO crashes and government cover-ups. The most famous cases of this kind are the Roswell UFO crash of 1947 and the Kecksburg, Pennsylvania UFO crash of 1965. Efforts by the United States government to investigate UFOs have included the United States Air Force's (**USAF**) well-known **Project Blue Book** and the **Area 51** story. All of this is explored and examined in this volume.

Are UFOs real? Are they friendly or hostile? What should one do upon seeing a UFO? This book answers all of these questions and more through an incredible journey exploring one of the most perplexing and persistent mysteries of modern times: aliens and UFOs.

Ancient Astronauts

It is thousands of years ago, and a small group of early humans cower in a cave. Suddenly, they look up to see a weird shiny object hovering above them. As they watch, the object lands, and a short figure with shiny clothing exits. After a few minutes, the creature returns to the object and departs. Afterwards, the amazed early humans are unable to fully understand the event. However, they do record the encounter in the only way they know how—with art.

While the above scenario is fictional, incidents like this may have actually provided the first evidence of early UFO visitations.

If there is one thing that ufologists are sure about, it's that UFOs have been visiting Earth for a long, long time. But the question remains: Exactly how long have they been here? This is not so easy to answer. It seems that the farther back one looks in time, the more clues there are to find.

To examine these clues, it is necessary to travel back in time thousands of years, to an era when humans were just beginning to learn the basics of civilization, including construction, agriculture, writing, and, most importantly here, art.

ANCIENT E.T. ART

Numerous ancient stone carvings, rock paintings, and mysterious monuments throughout the world hint that extraterrestrials (E.T.s) may have visited this planet in the distant past. Granite carvings in Hunan, Asia, for example, show human figures gazing into the sky at hovering, cylindrical objects on which other people are standing. These look much like today's UFO reports. The only problem is, these carvings are dated around 45,000 BCE!

Petroglyphs in Toro Muerto, Peru, show figures with large transparent helmets. These rock carvings are dated at about 11,000 BCE.

On the Tassili plateau in the Sahara Desert are sculpted rock figures, also with large, round heads, like helmets. These statues date back to around 6000 BCE.

Figures carved into rock in Lomoukai, Nambu Province in Africa depict figures in what appear to be modern spacesuits. These carvings are dated to around 4300 BCE.

Another example comes from the Australian Aborigines. Numerous ancient rock paintings depict short, robed figures with large staring eyes and huge helmet-like heads, again the typical description of an extraterrestrial. These images are known to be 3,000 years old.

More clues come from a wide variety of cultures. An early Colombian artifact looks almost exactly like the space shuttle. A clay sculpture from a pre-Japanese culture shows what looks like an astronaut inside a pressurized spacesuit. Both of these artifacts are at least 3,000 years old.

Why do so many different cultures across the world create these strange figures? Could aliens and UFOs have inspired them? Interestingly, many early cultures have myths and legends about wise God-like beings that came from the sky to teach humanity.

Mysterious places like Easter Island, Stonehenge, the Egyptian pyramids, and countless others have also generated years of debate about how they came to exist. While some researchers have speculated that extraterrestrials may have helped to construct these monuments, most modern researchers believe that humans built them. There are tantalizing clues, however, that some of these creations may have been inspired by visiting extraterrestrials.

One example that stands out above all the other places is a mysterious desert plateau in Nazca, Peru. This 500-square-mile volcanic plateau contains artwork by an unknown creator (or creators). There are hundreds of markings on the plateau—including animal figures such as monkeys, spiders, whales, and various birds, as well as geometric designs, patterns, and lines—that can only be seen from high up in the air.

These markings are more than 2,000 years old, predating both the Incan and Mayan empires. Therefore the question remains: Who made these markings that can only be seen from the air, and why? Could they have been inspired by extraterrestrials? The Nazca mystery remains unsolved.[1]

Figure 1.1 *These giant hands are part of the Nazca Lines in Peru.* (Kevin Schafer/Corbis)

UFOS IN ANCIENT EGYPT AND INDIA

Fortunately, there are more than just pictures and carvings that record early UFO visitations. On an ancient Egyptian papyrus dated from 1504 BCE is one of the earliest known written records of a UFO encounter. It was written during the reign of Egyptian pharaoh Thutmose III, and is now at the Egyptian museum at the Vatican. The hieroglyphics were translated by Egyptologists and tell an amazing story. One day a group of Egyptian citizens observed "a circle of fire that was coming from the sky." The people became frightened and threw themselves to the ground. A few days later, the strange objects returned. According to the document, "Now after some days had passed, these things became more numerous in the sky than ever. They shone more in the sky than the brightness of the sun, and extended to the limits of the four supports of the heavens . . . Powerful was the position of these fire circles."

Texts from Ancient India also provide suggestions of UFO activity. More than 5,000 years old and written in ancient Sanskrit, these texts describe flying ships, called *vimánas*, or sky-boats. Researcher Richard Thompson has studied hundreds of such accounts and writes that the *vimánas* have "many features reminiscent of UFOs." Early cultures might have had trouble understanding the phenomenon of UFOs, but they found the activity important enough to record. In each case the observers interpreted UFOs in the context of their own culture.[2]

BIBLICAL UFOS

Even the Bible mentions possible extraterrestrial encounters. The "Wheels of Ezekiel" described in the Bible contains many parallels to modern day UFO reports. The incident took place in 593 BCE and appears in the beginning of the New Testament. Ezekiel was alone when he saw a "a great cloud with brightness round about it, and fire flashing forth constantly, and in the midst of the fire, as it were gleaming bronze." Ezekiel also observed strange wheels within wheels and other details that sounded very much like a machine. Researcher Josef Blumrich wrote a book, *The Spaceships of Ezekiel* (1974), theorizing that Ezekiel encountered actual extraterrestrials.

Another example from the Bible is Elijah's ascension in a "chariot of fire." Some researchers speculate that the chariot of fire is actually a UFO. This has also led to speculation that some reports of angels may actually refer to extraterrestrials.

UFOS IN ROMAN TIMES

It wasn't until Roman times that historians began to keep detailed records of UFO encounters. Early Roman writer Julius Obsequens was one of the world's first UFO investigators. He began recording strange events in the year 222 BCE, when two Roman consuls observed "a great light, like day, at midnight, when three moons appeared in quarters of the sky distant from each other."

In 216 BCE, he wrote of another sighting: "Things like ships were seen in the sky over Italy . . . At Arpi, a round shield was seen in the sky . . . At Capua, the sky was all on fire, and one saw figures like ships."

Obsequens eventually recorded dozens of accounts, often referring to the strange objects as shields, ships, or burning torches—all objects that were familiar to people in Roman society at the time.

Another early researcher was German scholar Lycosthenes, who recorded numerous UFO sightings over Europe. The following account comes from the year 457 CE: "Over Brittany, France, a blazing thing like a globe was seen in the sky. Its size was immense, and on its beams hung a ball of fire like a dragon out of whose mouth proceeded two beams, one of which stretched beyond France, the other reached towards Ireland, and ended in fire, like rays."

In the year 796, "Small globes were seen circling around the sun."

And in the year 919, "A thing like a burning torch was seen in the sky, and glistening balls like stars moved to and fro in the air over Hungary."

Another sighting that cannot be easily explained occurred in 1168: "A globe of fire was seen moving to and fro in the air on 20 March."

Some of the early accounts match up perfectly with today's reports. In the year 1290, for example, the abbot and monks at Begeland Abbey in England observed a "flat, round, shining, silvery object" that flew over the abbey, causing "utmost terror."[3]

UFOS IN THE MIDDLES AGES

As history marched forward into the Middle Ages, accounts of UFO sightings became more detailed. In 1322: "In the first hour of the night of November 4 there was seen in the sky over Uxbridge, England a pillar of fire the size of a small boat, pallid and livid in colour. It rose from the south, crossed the sky with slow and grave motions, and went north. Out of the front of the pillar, a fervent red flame burst forth with great beams of light. Its speed increased, and it flew through the air."

In 1387, England experienced a wave of UFO activity when citizens observed "a fire in the sky, like a burning and revolving wheel, or round barrel of flame, emitting fire from above, and others in the shape of a long fiery beam."

On April 14, 1561, numerous residents of Nuremberg, Germany, saw hundreds of globes, cylinders, and other strange-shaped objects flying in darting patterns, as if fighting one another. The sighting lasted about an hour and was described by witnesses as a "very frightful spectacle." An unknown artist recorded the event in a woodcarving, which shows the strange fleet of flying objects, including a few actually crashing to the Earth.

On August 7, 1566, Samuel Coccius of Basel, England, wrote that at sunrise "many large black globes were seen in the air, moving before

IFOs, or Identified Flying Objects

It's a bird! It's a plane! No . . . it's a UFO! UFOs are not always what they seem. In fact, most ufologists agree that only about 10 percent of UFO reports are genuine "unknowns." The remaining 90 percent of the reports are caused by natural or human-made phenomena. Below is a list of the phenomena that are sometimes mistaken for UFOs:

- Venus or other planets
- meteorites, fireballs
- ball lightning
- weather balloons
- stars, comets
- airplanes, helicopters, and other conventional aircraft
- satellites, rockets, missiles, and other advanced military aircraft
- mirages caused by temperature inversions
- lenticular (saucer-shaped) clouds
- lights from buildings, searchlights, lighthouses, and other structures
- fireworks
- Aurora Borealis (Northern Lights)
- sundogs, which are atmospheric reflections from ice crystals
- birds, fireflies

the sun with great speed and turning against each other as if fighting." Coccius memorialized the event in a woodcarving, which shows about 40 objects filling the sky as stunned observers look on.

Many astronomers have seen UFOs. The famous English astronomer, Edmund Halley, who discovered Halley's comet, also claims to have seen a UFO. In May of 1677, he and numerous others observed a "great light in the sky all over southern England, many miles high." The light moved "with incredible speed, and was very bright. It seemed to vanish and left a pale white light behind it. There were no hissing sounds and no explosion." Was this a UFO or a meteor? Even Halley wasn't sure.

On July 9, 1686, German astronomer Gottfried Kirch observed a "burning globe" that was so bright "one could read without a candle." He used a telescope and estimated that the object was 30 miles up. After eight minutes, the light disappeared. Kirch later learned that other people eight miles away observed the same object earlier that evening.

Throughout the 1700s, the *Gentleman's Magazine* of England recorded numerous accounts, such as the following incredible sighting: "In March, 1719, and again on 29 August, 1738, there appeared in the sky over England at 3 P.M. in the northeast a glowing ball like a cone, with a jet of flame at the rear . . . It was like a cone of fire, ending in a sharp point, with a bright ball at the thicker end. The ball seemed to burst and go away in a jet of flame."

On January 2, 1749, three large spherical-shaped objects "like the moon" appeared over Japan, causing widespread riots. The government was forced to enact martial law to stop the panic.

During this time, several Renaissance painters created works of art that contained images of typical flying saucers. In 2003, researcher Matthew Hurley identified many examples. A fifteenth-century painting by Italian artist Ghirlandaio shows the Virgin Mary with a disk-shaped object hovering in the sky. In the background, a man points at the object. Another sixteenth-century fresco shows a figure inside a flying object that is darting across the sky above a crowd of people.[4]

UFOS IN THE 1800S

Sightings continued strong into the 1800s. In July 1868, residents of Copiago, Chile, observed an unidentified "aerial construction" fly overhead. It was described as having shiny scales and making a noise like a machine.

A dramatic account from the summer of 1883 was published in the West German magazine, *Der Stern*. According to the report, "All the children and the teacher in the public elementary school at Sege-berg, saw in the sky two fiery balls, the size of full moons, traveling side by side, not very swiftly, from north to south, on a clear and sunny day."

Despite the many sightings, most people still didn't view UFOs as aliens from space. More popular explanations included angels, demons, or signs from God or the Devil. At this time, humans had still not learned how to fly, so the idea of space-travel and life on other planets hadn't entered the public consciousness. It wouldn't be until airplanes and rockets were invented in the early twentieth century that people began to seriously consider that UFOs might be creatures from other planets.

Then in 1896, the United States experienced its first UFO wave when residents across northern California reported seeing an "airship" in the sky. The first sighting to gain widespread attention occurred on November 17, 1896. As reported in the *Sacramento Bee*: "Last evening between the hours of six and seven o'clock, in the year of our Lord 1896, a most startling exhibition was seen in the sky in this city of Sacramento. People standing on the sidewalks at certain points in the city between the hours stated, saw coming through the sky over the housetops what appeared to them to be merely an electric arc lamp propelled by some mysterious force. It came out of the east and sailed unevenly toward the southwest, dropping now nearer to the earth, and now suddenly rising into the air." Several witnesses said they heard voices. Among the many witnesses was the daughter of the mayor of Sacramento.

UFO Statistics

M any surveys have been taken to determine how many people believe in UFOs, or have seen them. The results may surprise you.

The Gallup Poll

Probably the most respected poll is the Gallup Poll. The results of Gallup polls concerning UFOs have been very consistent throughout the years, as evidenced in Table 1.1.

TABLE 1.1

Gallup Poll of UFO Believers and Sightings

Year	Percentage Who Believe in UFOs	Percentage Who Have Seen a UFO
1966	46%	5%
1973	53%	11%
1978	57%	9%
1987	49%	14%
2001	50%	10%

The Roper Poll

The United States has a population of about 300 million people. And if 10 percent of Americans have seen UFOs, that would equal 30 million UFO witnesses. This raises the question, how many people have been abducted by UFOs? Another prominent survey is the Roper Poll. In 1974, the Roper Poll found that 40 percent of Americans believe in UFOs. In 1996, however, the Roper Poll found that 2 percent of Americans have experienced a UFO abduction. If true, that would equal 6 million Americans who have been inside a UFO! These surveys tend to raise more questions that are difficult to answer; for example, with 30 million UFO witnesses, why is it that only half of the people surveyed even believe in UFOs? Also, with 6 million UFO **abductees**, why is it that there isn't more physical evidence?

Where are the UFOs?

What are the top three places in the United States for seeing UFOs? According to the National UFO Reporting Service (NUFORC), the top three spots are:

1 California

2 Washington

3 Texas

Nobody is sure why these spots are more active than others. California does have the highest population of any other state, and Texas is the second largest state. Both of these might be reasons, but at this point, the answer remains one of the many mysteries surrounding the subject of aliens and UFOs.

Over the next week, the mysterious airship continued to appear. Five days later, on November 22, 1896, dozens of passengers on an Oakland streetcar observed an object that looked like a "wingless cigar." The object emitted beams of light and traveled slowly overhead. Again, the account became front-page news.

Before long, the wave spread across the United States, with thousands of people reporting the strange zeppelin-like objects. In a few of the cases, witnesses encountered human-looking people who were dressed strangely and spoke unknown languages.

At first, people assumed that these airships were coming from foreign countries, such as Cuba. Again, the idea of aliens visiting Earth from outer space was still largely unknown. Today, the mysterious airship wave remains unexplained. Some researchers believe that the sightings may have been the result of early undercover experiments with dirigibles, zeppelins, and other airships. And in fact, only one year later, on November 3, 1897, timber merchant David Schwarz of the Austro-Hungarian Empire invented and successfully flew an airship.

Other researchers have a stranger explanation for the airship mystery. They say that UFOs are actually putting on different masks for each culture, and may actually be some sort of interdimensional visitors and not extraterrestrials at all. The best evidence for this theory is the fact that UFOs do seem to appear different in each culture. For example, the many cases of fairies and elves in the medieval times may have been actual fairies and elves, actual aliens that people just thought were fairies or elves, or perhaps another mask worn by the interdimensional beings. Explanations for these phenomena are not always easy.[5]

"FOO FIGHTERS"

During the middle of World War II in 1943 and 1944, numerous fighter pilots began to see what they called "foo fighters," or small balls of light that followed their aircraft. At first, everyone assumed that the balls of light were secret German weapons. However, it was later discovered that German and Japanese pilots also encountered the strange balls of light and thought they were American or English secret weapons. Neither thought that they were extraterrestrials.

Strangely, the foo fighters never attacked the planes, but instead flew behind them or whirled around them in curious patterns. They appeared alone or in groups. The United States military and the British military both launched investigations, but were unable to account for the strange sightings.[6]

THE SWEDISH GHOST ROCKETS

Only one year later, UFOs came back with a vengeance. Starting in May 1946, Sweden and other northern European countries were plagued by a wave of "ghost rockets." Described as missiles, spheres, fireballs, cigar-shaped, and football shaped, these objects moved in typical UFO patterns, racing at high speeds, darting at sharp angles,

Figure 1.2 *During World War II, many airplane pilots saw small balls of light called foo fighters chasing their planes. This photograph shows two foo fighters accompanying a flight of Japanese fighters over the Suzuka Mountains in central Japan.* (Mary Evans Picture Library)

and hovering or floating. By the end of 1946, more than 1,000 reports of the objects came from Sweden alone. The objects, however, were seen all across Europe and even in Africa and India. By 1947, there were 2,000 reports, including a few citing explosions or landings. There was no evidence, however, of any injuries to people, nor was anyone able to recover one of the objects. The Swedish Defense Ministry launched an investigation, believing that the objects were probably secret Soviet weapons. Their research showed that at least 200 of the reports were unexplained and "cannot be the phenomena of nature or the products of imagination."[7]

From ancient times up to 1947, mainstream society still had not faced the possibility that Earth was being visited by extraterrestrials. However, something was about to happen that would change everything.

The Sighting That Changed the World

On June 24, 1947, the world changed forever. It was a sunny afternoon as private pilot and businessman Kenneth Arnold flew his small plane over Mount Rainier in Washington State. He was part of a rescue mission to search for another plane that had crashed in the local mountains. Suddenly a "tremendously bright flash" in the air caught his eye. To Arnold's amazement, he observed nine strange metallic objects skipping "like saucers" across the sky. As an experienced pilot, he could tell that they were like "no aircraft I had ever seen before." He watched them for about two minutes, as they performed amazing maneuvers. Arnold estimated that the objects were moving at more than 1,700 miles per hour!

When he landed, Arnold reported his sighting to officials. Military officers interviewed him and concluded that the sighting was unexplained. The media heard about the case, and Arnold's sighting became front-page news across the world. The story electrified the public. For the first time, the world was introduced to the word "flying saucer." Earth, it appeared, was being visited by beings from outer space! The Modern Age of UFOs had begun.[8]

Arnold's sighting was only the tip of the iceberg. Now that a credible witness had reported seeing UFOs, the floodgates opened for hundreds of other people across the world to report their own sightings. The summer of 1947 went down in history as one of the busiest years of UFO activity ever recorded. And ever since 1947, UFOs have been reported every year.

Most of the sightings involved metallic disks that hovered silently, moved at right angles, and traveled at supersonic speeds. These objects were seen by large groups of people across the United States and the world. Only a few of these incidents are known as "classic cases." What follows are some of the world's best classic UFO cases.

"FLIER DIES CHASING A FLYING SAUCER"

On January 8, 1948, flying saucers again became front-page news when an Air Force Pilot was killed while in pursuit of an unknown object over Kentucky. The ordeal began on January 7, when the sheriff's station of Louisville, Kentucky, received several calls from local residents reporting a strange circular object, about 250 feet in diameter, moving over the town. Witnesses described the object as "glowing" or "metallic." The local Godman Air Force Base was alerted, but they denied any knowledge of the object. Then, a few minutes later, the base's tower operators were shocked to see the unknown object hovering over the base itself!

The UFO remained in view for 45 minutes while numerous base officials observed it through binoculars. Finally, they decided to scramble jets to pursue the unknown object.

At the time of the sighting, Captain Thomas J. Mantell and his team were approaching Godman AFB in four F-51 fighter jets. Captain Mantell was ordered to intercept and identify the object. Air traffic controllers guided him towards the location of the UFO. Fifteen minutes later, Mantell made visual contact. He radioed to the base, "I see something above and ahead of me."

The control tower remained silent while Mantell continued to comment. "I've sighted the thing. It looks metallic and it's tremendous in size . . . Now it's starting to climb."

The young pilot increased his throttles and climbed in altitude to about 20,000 feet. He radioed that he was closing in on the object, and then came silence. There were no more messages from Mantell. The wreckage of his plane was found shortly later. For some reason that would never be explained, the plane had gone out of control and plunged to the earth. Mantell died instantly upon impact.

The press went wild. The *New York Times* printed the headline, "Flier Dies Chasing a 'Flying Saucer.'" Military officials attempted to downplay the sighting, saying that Mantell had mistaken Venus for a UFO and that he simply ran out of oxygen and crashed. While it is true that Mantell's plane was not equipped with oxygen, at the time of the sighting, Venus was low on the horizon and could not have been responsible for the object. When this fact became clear, skeptics then claimed that Mantell was chasing a large Skyhook weather balloon.

Believers, on the other hand, say that the UFO may have zapped his plane out of the sky. There are many cases during which UFOs affect electronic equipment; these are discussed in later chapters. There were also rumors that the wreckage of Mantell's plane showed evidence of unusual damage, though this was never confirmed. To this day, the truth remains unknown.[9]

UFO OVER FARGO

Many pilots have reported seeing UFOs. For some reason, UFOs are attracted to other flying objects—including normal planes. A similar and equally dramatic airplane-UFO encounter occurred just two months later over Fargo, North Dakota. Twenty-five year old George Gorman was a jet pilot and second lieutenant of the North Dakota Air National Guard. On the evening of October 1, 1948, Gorman was coming in for a landing at Fargo Airport when he noticed a weird, glowing disk-shaped object below and ahead of him. As he watched, the unknown object steadied its flight, then pulled into a sharp left turn heading toward the airport control tower.

Where is the Proof?

If UFOs are real, where is the evidence? Is there any actual proof of UFOs? In fact, there are many different kinds of evidence that ufologists have gathered to support the case for the UFO. Below is a list of some of the major types of UFO evidence, all of which is examined in this book.

- **Eyewitness testimony**: This is best when supported by multiple witnesses and lie detector tests.

- **Photographs and moving films**: Photos and films are great evidence, but they must be carefully analyzed to rule out hoaxing.

- **Radar returns**: This type of evidence is rare but has been reported by both commercial and military pilots and ground radar.

- **Landing traces**: There are more than 2,000 cases where UFOs have left evidence of landing, including marks in the ground or even burns.

- **Electromagnetic effects**: UFOs often affect machinery including cars, radios, televisions, and more.

- **Medical effects**: There are about 400 cases of UFO injuries and 150 cases of UFO healings.

- **Metal fragments**: In a few rare cases, UFOs have left metal samples behind that seem to defy analysis.

- **Alien implants**: Recent analysis of small "foreign bodies" found in the bodies of abductees shows that these objects might be extraterrestrial.

- **Animal reactions**: Many cases exist of animals reacting to UFOs.

Figure 2.1   *A formation of UFOs photographed by a U.S. Coast Guard cameraman in Salem, Massachusetts.* (Bettmann/Corbis)

- **Historical accounts**: Evidence of ancient E.T.s exists in many cultures.

- **Government documents**: Thousands of pages of official UFO documents have been released through the **Freedom of Information Act**.

Gorman realized instantly he was seeing something unusual and decided to take action. Little did he know, he was about to make UFO history. "I dived after it . . . but I couldn't catch up with the thing. It started gaining altitude and again made a left bank. I put my F-51 into a sharp turn and tried to cut off the light, in my turn. By then we were at 7,000 feet. Suddenly, the thing made a sharp turn right and we were headed straight for each other! Just when we were about to collide, I guess I got scared. I went into a dive and the light passed over my canopy at about 500 feet. Then the thing made a left circle about 1,000 feet above me, and I gave chase again."

Meanwhile, the air traffic controller, L.D. Jensen, was shocked to observe the entire "cat and mouse" fight between the pilot and the UFO. He grabbed a pair of binoculars. While he could clearly identify Gorman's plane, the lighted object remained unidentifiable. Several other witnesses in the area also observed the strange object. For the next half-hour, Gorman chased the object, reaching speeds up to 400 miles per hour. The object easily eluded him and finally sped away, never to reappear.

After the encounter, Air Force investigators from Project Blue Book interviewed Gorman. Project Blue Book was responsible for investigating UFO reports for the Air Force. At the time of the incident, the U.S. Air Force had taken a policy of ridiculing UFO encounters, usually explaining them away as hallucinations, hoaxes, or misperceptions. They concluded that Gorman had encountered a weather balloon. The case was widely published in the media, and again skeptics and believers were divided. Like many UFO encounters, there was little evidence other than eyewitness testimony. Gorman, however, remains unshaken in his convictions and says, "I am convinced there was thought behind the thing's maneuvers. I had the distinct impression that its maneuvers were controlled by thought or reason."[10]

One of the common misconceptions about UFO encounters is that they are very rare. In fact, each year produces a number of high-quality reports. Only a very few of these cases, however, are reported in the popular media. One of the next classic UFO cases to grab the attention of the world is known today as the "Lubbock Lights."

THE LUBBOCK LIGHTS

It all began on the evening of August 25, 1951, in Lubbock, Texas. A scientist from the Atomic Energy Commission and his wife were in the yard of their home. Suddenly, both noticed an enormous, silent, V-shaped aircraft dart overhead at an altitude of less than 1,000 feet. The craft was covered with colored lights and strange markings.

Unknown to the couple, other witnesses in the area were also seeing strange objects. The next report came from another group of scientists including a geologist, two engineers, and a physicist, each of who observed a formation of nearly three-dozen unidentified turquoise lights moving quickly overhead from north to south. A few hours later, another fleet of UFOs flew over the group of scientists in an unorganized cluster. The "Lubbock Lights" case had begun!

The couple and the group of scientists reported their sighting to the Air Force, which began an investigation. The Air Force found further confirmation for the sighting when the nearby radar station of the Air Defense Command Network reported that they observed the unknown objects on their radarscopes and clocked them at a speed of 900 miles per hour.

The group of scientists was amazed by their two sightings, and they conjectured that the UFOs might return. They decided to conduct a UFO stakeout. To their amazement, the UFOs did return, again and again! Over the next month, the group of scientists (which had added two more members) experienced a series of 12 different sightings. In each of these cases, the objects were totally silent, moved at supersonic speeds, and sometimes turned at right angles.

Meanwhile, in the town of Lubbock itself, more than 200 concerned citizens also viewed the unusual aerial display. On August 31,

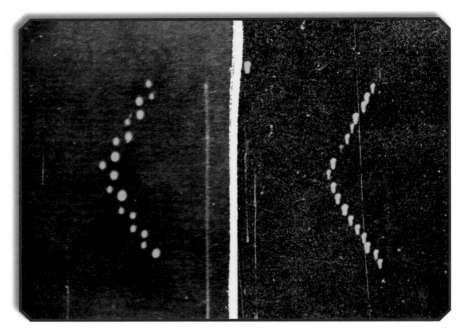

Figure 2.2 *The Lubbock Lights. In August of 1951, the town of Lubbock, Texas experienced a wave of UFO activity. On August 31, resident Carl Hart Jr. snapped this famous photograph of a formation of objects as they passed over the town. The photograph has never been satisfactorily explained.* (Bettmann/Corbis)

1951, resident and amateur photographer Carl Hart Jr. saw the objects. He grabbed his Kodak camera and quickly snapped two clear photographs of the glowing UFOs, both of which showed the formation of unusual craft.

Major Edward Ruppelt, the head of Project Blue Book, wrote of the case, "This was by far the best combination of UFO reports I'd ever read, and I'd read every one in the Air Force's files."

Still there was little that could be done. By the end of August, the UFOs had stopped appearing and the weird wave of sightings came to a sudden end.[11]

While the Lubbock Lights made for an amazing case, a far more dazzling case was about to occur, this time directly over the nation's capital. One of the most common questions asked about UFOs is, "If UFOs are real, why don't they land on the White House lawn and make an official announcement?" In the summer of 1952, this very nearly happened.

THE WASHINGTON NATIONALS

On July 19, 1952, at 11:40 P.M., air traffic controller Edward Nugent at Washington National Airport spotted seven unusual-looking blips on his radarscope. Nugent watched in amazement as the blips performed amazing maneuvers, traveling up to 7,000 miles per hour. He immediately called the senior air traffic controller Harry Barnes.

Barnes looked at the scope in shock. In a later interview, Barnes said, "We knew immediately that a very strange situation existed . . . there is no other conclusion that I can reach but that for six hours there were at least 10 unidentified flying objects moving above Washington. They were not ordinary aircraft. I could tell that by their movement on the scope. I can safely deduce that they performed gyrations which no known aircraft can perform. By this I mean that our scopes showed that they could make right angle turns and complete reversals of flight."

Barnes immediately contacted nearby Andrews Air Force Base who also had unusual blips on their radar. Later, they made visual contact with the UFOs. Airman William Brady was the first to see "an object which looked like an orange ball of fire, trailing a tail."

Following Brady's sighting, numerous other officers, guards, and employees observed the UFOs. Meanwhile, airline pilots throughout the area called in to report UFOs cavorting around their own planes. When the activity continued, commercial jets were grounded and Newcastle Air Force Base sent out two F-49 jet interceptors to chase the unknown objects. Each time the jets approached, however, the UFOs would dart away. When the jets left, the UFOs returned.

The sightings continued all night, and were seen by hundreds of witnesses over a widespread area. The next day, a press conference was held, and the Air Force attempted to explain the sightings. The public was told that the objects were illusions caused by "temperature inversions" in the atmosphere. Fortunately, the sightings were so numerous that they were impossible to cover up or explain away. Today, the sightings are believed by most researchers to be entirely valid and are considered one of the classic cases of UFO history. Researcher Captain Kevin Randle (U.S. Air Force) wrote a full-length book about the sightings. Says Randle, "The evidence is that something extraordinary was seen in the sky over Washington. Radar confirmed the sightings and fighters attempted to intercept these objects. There were visual sightings. And there was pressure by the Air Force to force their personnel to change their descriptions of the UFOs and their conclusions about the objects. We can say with certainty that something was seen by radar and observed visually . . . If the objects sighted were manufactured craft, then it is clear that they hadn't been built on this planet because of their speed and maneuverability. The only explanation that fits the facts is the extra-terrestrial. The Washington Nationals show that we have been visited. There is no other plausible explanation."[12]

With the dramatic Washington sightings, public interest in UFOs soared. In fact, some researchers believe that the UFOs were actually putting on a display and announcing their presence. And it wasn't long before more high-quality cases began to occur, making it very difficult for the Air Force to debunk the sightings. One of the next best-verified cases occurred over Ann Arbor, Michigan.

SWAMP SIGHTING

On March 18, 1966, 50 or more witnesses (including a dozen police officers) observed a large, disk-shaped craft hovering low over the marshlands outside of Ann Arbor, Michigan. Several witnesses reported seeing four other smaller objects escorting the larger one.

UFOs Among the Stars

UFOs are reported by all kinds of people, regardless of age, sex, race, religion, or education. The only requirement for seeing a UFO is looking up at the right time. In fact, many famous people have reported their own UFO encounters:

- Future president Jimmy Carter and several other people were in Georgia in 1973 when they observed a large glowing object in the sky. Says Carter, "It was 30 degrees above the horizon and looked about as large as the moon." The object darted around for a few minutes and disappeared. Carter later reported his sighting to the Center For UFO Studies.

- Astronaut James McDivitt photographed a UFO while orbiting the earth in the Gemini 5 space capsule. Says McDivitt, "From what I could tell, the object resembled a beer can with a cylinder protruding from the top of it." McDivitt turned the photos over to NASA, who never returned them.

- On August 23, 1973, singer/songwriter John Lennon was in his high-rise apartment on New York's Manhattan Island, when he and his girlfriend, Mae Pang, both observed a "large circular object . . . shaped like a flattened cone" cruise slowly past their balcony. Lennon called the police, who told them that they had already received dozens of calls reporting the same UFO.

- World-famous boxer Muhammad Ali claims to have seen UFOs on several occasions, usually star-like objects. Says Ali, "The closest one happened when a cigar-shaped ship hovered briefly over a car I was a passenger in . . . What a sight that was."

- Sammy Davis Jr. observed several UFOs in Palm Springs, California. Says Davis, "First they would stand still, and then they would take off and stop again, before finally shooting away in a flash."

Over the next three days, dozens of other residents and more police officers also viewed the object as it hovered over the marshes. The Air Force was alerted, but denied any knowledge of the case.

As if angry at being ignored, the UFOs returned with a vengeance. The next day, on March 22, 1966, more than 80 students at Hillsdale College observed a large, unknown glowing object move in darting patterns over the Ann Arbor swamplands. Also present were civil defense authority William Van Horn and Kelly Hearn, journalist and dean of Hillsdale College. When the UFO refused to leave, the police were called and officers viewed the craft. As the crowd watched, the UFO seemed to show off its ability to maneuver quickly around the area. Van Horn observed the object through binoculars and told reporters, "It was definitely some kind of vehicle."

By now, the Michigan sightings had become front-page news across the nation. The Air Force could no longer safely ignore the situation and sent their astronomical consultant, J. Allen Hynek, to investigate. After almost no investigation, Hynek held a press conference and announced that the sightings were probably caused by "swamp gas." The public became outraged and the Air Force was accused of trying to cover up the sightings. J. Allen Hynek, who had previously sided with the Air Force, began to wonder if perhaps he had made a mistake. He later left the Air Force and wrote two best-selling books about the UFO phenomenon, criticizing the Air Force's policy of debunking good cases, and stating without any doubt that UFOs are real.[13]

POLICE CHASE

Meanwhile, the cases continued. Less than one month later, two Ohio police officers would become the center of a huge controversy following their incredible encounter with a UFO on a lonely road late at night. Many witnesses regret seeing a UFO not because of the E.T.s, but because of how society reacts. These two police officers learned this the hard way. The ordeal began just before dawn on April 17, 1966, when deputies Dale Spaur and Wilbur Neff were alerted by their local station to be on the lookout for a UFO that was reportedly heading in their direction. Moments later, the officers were shocked to see a 50-foot wide, metallic saucer-shaped object with a dome on top. They could hear no noise except for a soft hum. The object glowed brightly and sent down a powerful beam of light. Said Spaur, "I had never seen anything this bright before in my life."

The officers radioed to their superiors that they had the UFO in sight. The dispatcher told them to keep the object in view while he sent another squad car with camera equipment.

At that point, the UFO began to move east toward Pennsylvania. Officers Spaur and Neff followed the object. Soon, they were racing along at more than 90 miles per hour. Incredibly, whenever they fell behind the UFO, it appeared to slow down and wait for them. Meanwhile, other officers had also sighted the object and joined the chase.

The UFO continued to play a cat-and-mouse game with the police officers, eventually leading them nearly 90 miles away. At this point, the officers were running low on gas and had to give up the chase. They notified Pittsburgh Airport, who said that they had picked the object up on radar, though this was later denied.

Meanwhile, news reporters had been monitoring police transmissions and knew about the whole encounter. So, when deputies Spaur and Neff returned to their station, the reporters were already waiting. The encounter became front-page news. The Air Force sent Blue Book officers to investigate. They concluded that the officers had only been chasing the planet Venus! The explanation caused public outrage. A judge and former congressman called the explanation "ridiculous." Ohio Congressman William Stanton said, "The Air Force has failed in its responsibility." Even Project Blue Book consultant J. Allen Hynek disagreed with the Air Force's explanation.

Unfortunately, deputies Spaur and Neff were ridiculed mercilessly, and both eventually lost their jobs. Says Spaur, "If I could change all that I have done in my life, I would change just one thing, and that would be the night we chased that damn saucer."

Neff agreed, "If that thing landed in my backyard, I wouldn't tell a soul."[14]

By now, so many encounters were occurring that the media couldn't keep up. Numerous citizen UFO groups formed such as the National Investigative Committee of Aerial Phenomenon (NICAP) and the Aerial Phenomenon Research Organization (APRO), both of which collected and studied literally thousands of cases. Meanwhile, the Air Force's Project Blue Book was followed by several other governmental investigations. At the same time, there was a change in the UFO phenomenon itself. In the 1940s and 1950s, there were many sightings over power stations, military bases, and other technological installations. Investigators Coral and Jim Lorenzen successfully predicted sightings that occurred over many such bases. However, in the 1960s and 1970s, the phenomenon began to escalate. For the first time, widespread reports came in of UFOs landing and strange-looking figures exiting the craft. After this came reports of abductions, also called *close encounters of the third kind*. Some of these amazing cases are covered in later chapters, but the 1970s and beyond brought many more incredible sightings worth investigating.

The early 1970s produced only scattered high-profile sightings. In 1973, however, a large wave of UFO activity hit the United States. One case that stands out above the rest is known as the Coyne Encounter.

THE COYNE ENCOUNTER

On the evening of October 18, 1973, Captain Lawrence Coyne and his crew of three Army officers were on a routine training flight in a helicopter over Columbus, Ohio. Suddenly Captain Coyne noticed a red light from the east, coming directly towards them. Says Coyne, "I looked to my right, through the right window, and I observed the light coming at a very fast speed, in excess of 600 knots."

Coyne attempted to radio nearby Mansfield Airport, but he got no reply. He put the helicopter into an emergency dive and all four officers braced for impact. Instead, they suddenly became enveloped in an eerie, bright red light. Looking up, they could see the object was hovering 500 feet directly overhead. The UFO then shined down a green beam of light on the men, and seconds later it zoomed away. As the UFO left, Captain Coyne realized his helicopter was being beamed upwards at a rate of 1,000 feet per second. He regained control and leveled out at 3,500 feet. Six minutes after the UFO left, their radio again began to function, and they returned to base. Unknown to the officers, witnesses on the ground also observed the entire incident. The case was later thoroughly investigated and no explanation was found. To this day, the incident remains unexplained.[15]

BLACK DUST

One of the most unique encounters from the 1980s occurred on the Nullabor Plain, in a remote area of Australia. On January 20, 1988, the Knowles family, including Fay Knowles and her three sons and their two dogs, drove along a desolate road at around 4:00 a.m. when they saw a strange light ahead of them on the highway. At first they thought it was a large truck, but as they approached, they realized it was a large egg-shaped object that gave off an intense white light. As the Knowles family drove by, the strange object started to pace their car. Then it started to maneuver around the car, nearly causing them to have an accident. At one point, the object seemed to leave, but then suddenly, the unthinkable happened. The object returned and actually landed on top of the car!

The family heard a loud clunking noise and felt the car shake. Suddenly, the entire vehicle was lifted up off the road. Mrs. Knowles reached out her window and touched the object, which she said felt "spongy and rubbery." She pulled her hand back in, and it was covered with strange black dust. Suddenly, the entire car filled with the black

Figure 2.3 *In 1988, the Knowles family of Australia encountered a UFO that landed on top of their car and lifted it up into the air.* (Kesara Art)

dust. At the same time, the Knowles heard a loud humming noise and the dogs started to panic. The family then felt very disoriented, as if time had slowed down. They found it difficult to speak or be heard by each other.

After a few moments, the car slammed back down onto the pavement, popping one of the rear tires. Fay Knowles brought the car to a screeching stop, and the family fled. Meanwhile, the UFO remained above the car for a few moments and then darted away.

Unknown to the Knowles, a trucker just a few miles down the highway also observed the strange object as it sent down what appeared to be beams of white light.

The Knowles family was extremely traumatized and the police were notified. Somehow the media heard about the sensational case and the Knowles became overnight, reluctant celebrities. Despite the physical evidence of their encounter (including strange indentations on the roof of their vehicle and the weird black dust), the family was ridiculed intensely in the press. Although they never backed down or changed their story, they later said that they regretted coming forward because of how they were treated.[16]

THE PHOENIX LIGHTS

One of the most widely viewed UFO sightings in history occurred on the evening of March 13, 1997, over the city of Phoenix, Arizona. For several weeks, strange lights had been seen over the area. But on March 13, a massive black triangular-shaped craft flew at low altitude over the city and was viewed by commercial pilots, air traffic controllers, police officers, and *thousands* of puzzled citizens. The object was videotaped and photographed. The "Phoenix Lights" stunned the nation. Where normally most UFOs seemed to hide, this UFO apparently wanted to be seen.

Concerned witnesses called up nearby Luke Air Force Base, but personnel there denied having any information about the sighting. Air

Force officials then refused to investigate. The controversy exploded, and theories ranged from military flares to secret military craft. Author and researcher Lynn Kitei, M.D., collected hundreds of testimonies and launched an extensive investigation. Her book, *The Phoenix Lights*, chronicles the entire event. Writes Kitei, "When the display came over the mountains of North Phoenix and moved over the city, thousands of people saw it. The route the mysterious lights took that night can be followed by tracking the 911 calls that came into the Phoenix police departments . . . Obviously something spectacular happened on the evening of March 13, 1997, throughout Arizona, but what?" Unfortunately, as with most UFO stories, the mystery remains.[17]

A WIDESPREAD SIGHTING

One of the most exciting and recent sightings occurred on January 5, 2000, over central Illinois. It all began at 4:00 a.m. when trucker Melvern Noll of Highland, Illinois, saw a strange object float overhead. He said it looked "like a two-story house . . . it had white lights and red blinking lights." Noll saw that the UFO was heading toward the city of Lebanon, so he called the Lebanon police department. Officer Ed Barton was dispatched to the scene and was shocked to see the UFO hovering at a low altitude over the city. Barton radioed the sheriff's station and told them he had the object in sight. Said Barton, "It's not the moon and it's not a star."

Meanwhile, other police officers were monitoring the radio frequencies. Six miles southwest, a police officer in Shiloh reported to his station that he too could see the UFO. Thirteen miles further southwest in Millstadt, police officer Craig Stevens went looking for the UFO and found it moving slowly over the city. Stevens radioed his superiors, telling them, "It's huge . . . it's kind of V-shaped." He jumped out of his squad car and quickly snapped a photograph.

Figure 2.4 *UFOs come in many different shapes and sizes. Here are some of the shapes of UFOs reported by eyewitnesses around the world.* (Kesara Art)

More citizens also reported seeing the UFO. When newspaper reporters discovered that so many police officers saw the UFO, the sighting became front-page news. Researchers later conducted a full-scale investigation. While the most popular explanation was that the UFO was a secret military aircraft from nearby Scott Air Force Base, officials at the base denied any involvement and said that their airport and control tower were actually closed at the time of the sighting.

Why do UFOs sometimes hide, and sometimes seem to want to be seen? Some researchers feel that the E.T.s are trying to get humanity used to their presence. Others say that humanity is not ready for open, official contact, and that is why the UFOs show themselves only briefly. As is often the case with UFOs, there are more questions than answers.[18]

3

When UFOs Land

Just after sunset on September 12, 1952, several children playing outside their homes in Flatwoods, Virginia, saw a bright flaming object move across the sky and suddenly land on a nearby hill a half mile away. When the weird glowing object stayed there, six of the children decided to get closer. They started the 15-minute hike to the landing spot. Along the way, two of the boys, Edison and Freddie May, stopped at their house and told their mother that they were going with their friends to see a landed flying saucer. Their mother, Kathleen May, was skeptical, abut also curious. She said, "You're not going by yourself!" It was just getting dark, so she grabbed a flashlight and joined the boys.

By now it was already dark. The group of six children and one adult crept towards the glowing object. As they approached, they could see that the object was sphere-shaped, and was pulsating with light. The whole area around the craft was foggy. Whatever it was, it wasn't normal.

Suddenly, one of the children thought he saw something glowing in one of the trees just ahead of them. Kathleen May shined her flashlight up and everybody screamed. Floating in front of them was a 12-foot tall robotic-looking creature with glowing red eyes, a teardrop-shaped head, and a cylindrical body with antennae coming out of the sides. Says Freddie May, "It was big . . . it was scary."

Figure 3.1 *On September 12, 1952, a group of six children and one adult encountered this 12-foot tall robotic creature hovering next to a landed UFO on a hilltop in Flatwoods, Virginia.* (Kesara Art)

The strange creature also gave off a horrible stench. As soon as May shined the flashlight on the creature, beams of light came out of its eyeballs and it "lit up like a Christmas tree." Then it floated quickly toward the frightened witnesses.

Everybody turned and ran down the hill screaming. Nobody looked back as they fled back into their homes. Kathleen May quickly called the police, and investigators instantly converged on the scene. They found strange markings on the ground and a strange odor still hung in the air. The media picked up the story and the case soon became widely known. To this day, nobody has been able to explain the incident of the Flatwoods Monster.

A simple sighting of a UFO is called a close encounter of the first kind. A close encounter of the second kind is when a UFO physically affects the environment, such as causing a car's engine to stall. However, what happens when UFOs land and aliens exit the craft? These cases are termed close encounters of the third kind. There have been literally thousands of reported UFO landings across the world. More than 2,000 of these cases involve physical trace evidence of the landing. The Flatwoods Monster case is only one example. Many other equally shocking cases exist. What makes landing cases so interesting is that they make the usual Air Force explanations of misperception or hallucination much harder to accept. These UFOs are no longer even UFOs; they are unidentified *landed* objects. For the first time, people were getting a good look at who was piloting these UFOs.[19]

THE BRUSH CREEK UFO LANDING

In February of 1953, miners John Van Black and John Allen were working outside their titanium mine near Brush Creek, California, when they saw a "metallic saucer" hovering over the area of the mine. During the next four weeks, the saucer returned four times. It was obvious to the men that the object was interested in their titanium mine.

On May 20, Black saw the familiar-looking saucer hovering about 200 feet above the creek next to the mine. After the object left, Black found several strange, five-inch footprints around the area.

One month later, on June 20, Black approached the area when he saw what he thought was a small child with a bucket. Looking closer, he saw it was a small man wearing green pants, unusual shoes, a jacket, and a green cap. He was very pale and had black hair. Says Black, "He looked like someone who had never been out in the sun much."

Black watched as the man scooped up water with a strange cone-shaped bucket. The figure then heard Black approaching and ran back into the saucer, which promptly took off and disappeared.

Black reported the event to the police. The story was leaked to the press and crowds of people showed up at the mine, hoping that the UFO would return again. Unfortunately, it never did, and the Brush Creek UFO landing remains a mystery. It seems clear, however, that the UFO was interested in the titanium mine.[20]

THE QUAROUBLE, FRANCE UFO LANDING

Some UFO cases impress investigators because they involve convincing physical evidence. On the evening of September 10, 1954, factory-worker Marius Dewilde of France was about to make UFO history. He went outside to investigate why his dog was barking. To his surprise, he could see a large, strangely shaped object had landed on the railroad tracks behind his home. Suddenly, he heard footsteps approaching. He grabbed his flashlight and shined it toward the sound.

To his shock, he saw "two creatures such as I had never seen before." The figures were each three feet tall, with large helmets and "one-piece outfits like the divers wear." Realizing that the figures weren't human, Dewilde turned to chase them. At that point, a beam of light shot out of the object on the railroad and hit Dewilde. As he says, "I closed my eyes and tried to yell, but I couldn't. It was just as if I had been paralyzed. I tried to move, but my legs wouldn't obey me."

The strange figures ran back into the object. The beam of light went out and the craft took off straight up and disappeared. Dewilde went straight to the police and reported his encounter. At first the police didn't believe him. But then more reports of sightings and landings in the area came in.

First the police and then the French Air Force decided to investigate. They returned to the area and were shocked to find that the wooden railroad ties where the UFO landed had deep impressions on the surface, as if they had supported a heavy weight. Research later showed that the object must have weighed about 30 tons! Also, the gravel in the area had been exposed to extremely high temperatures. Today, the case remains a classic "landing trace" case, and is still unexplained.[21]

THE HOPKINSVILLE GOBLINS

One of the most amazing close encounter cases of all times occurred on the evening of August 22, 1955. The Sutton family of Hopkinsville, Kentucky, was minding their own business when a "spaceship" landed in their backyard. Moments later, a short figure with large eyes, huge elephant-like ears, and a slit-like mouth appeared. It had long arms and legs and was dressed in silvery clothing. Frank Sutton quickly grabbed a shotgun and fired at the creature.

The bullet appeared to hit the creature, but it just fell down and got back up and ran away. They crept outside to investigate when suddenly the creature appeared on the roof of the house and grabbed at one of the family members. They shot at the creature again, but it just floated slowly down and scampered away.

Meanwhile, more of the strange creatures appeared and began to creep around the house, appearing and disappearing. Finally, the Suttons had enough. They piled into their car and raced to the police station. The police were amazed to see an entire family who were obviously shaken up and scared by something. They returned to investigate. As they approached, they saw a strange "lighted object" dart away. However, the creatures were gone.

This case is interesting because it shows just how varied the many different E.T.s are. While many reports of extraterrestrials can be categorized into various types, many other cases seem to involve totally unique E.T.s. The Hopkinsville goblins are a perfect example. Coral and Jim Lorenzen of the Aerial Phenomenon Research Organization (APRO) later researched the case. They found the witnesses credible and concluded that the family had seen something not from this world.[22]

THE SOCORRO INCIDENT

On April 24, 1964, a New Mexico police officer named Lonnie Zamora was chasing a speeding car down the highway when he saw a white flame in the distance and heard a strange explosion. He decided that he better investigate, so he stopped chasing the speeder and began to drive towards the source of the disturbance.

As he approached the area, he was shocked to see something literally out of this world. A giant, white egg-shaped object with a strange symbol on the side had just landed in a field. Standing next to the craft were two short humanoid figures about the size of "a young boy or a small adult" dressed in weird white jumpsuits. The two figures quickly climbed into the craft, which took off with a roaring flame. Officer Zamora hid behind his squad car as the craft roared overhead and disappeared into the sky.

Zamora quickly alerted the other officers and an official investigation followed. The United States Air Force and the **FBI** both investigated the case. At the landing site, they discovered several deep impressions in the ground. There was also a dark burned section where the craft had taken off. Finally, strange metal samples were recovered from the site. NASA scientist Dr. Henry Frankel conducted an analysis of the metal and found that it was composed of an unusual alloy of zinc and iron. Incredibly, this alloy could not have been made on

Types of E.T.s

*O*ne of the most shocking things about UFOs is the huge variety of different E.T.s. There are literally hundreds of different kinds of E.T.s reported. Fortunately, investigators have narrowed the reports down to a few main categories.

1 **Grays**: Three to five feet in height, large dark eyes, large hairless heads, small facial features. May be two different types, short and tall. Believed to originate from **Zeta-Reticuli**.

2 **Nordics**: Six feet in height, human-looking, blond hair, muscular bodies—could pass for human. May originate from the Pleiades.

3 **Praying Mantis**: Six to eight feet in height, with an appearance like a giant grasshopper or praying mantis insect. Origins unknown.

4 **Reptilion**: Six to nine feet in height with an appearance like a giant lizard. Also known as Reptoids. Theorized to originate from inner earth.

5 **Dwarfs**: Also known as short humanoids, three to four feet tall, sometimes human-looking, strong, sometimes hairy.

6 **Tall Humanoids**: Seven to nine feet in height, human-looking, though with larger eyes and sometimes hairless heads. Very rarely reported.

7 **Robots**: Three to 12 feet in height, variously described as metallic with colored lights, often in the shape of a person or cylinder.

earth, and the scientist concluded, "This finding definitely strengthens the case that might be made for an extraterrestrial origin of the Socorro object."

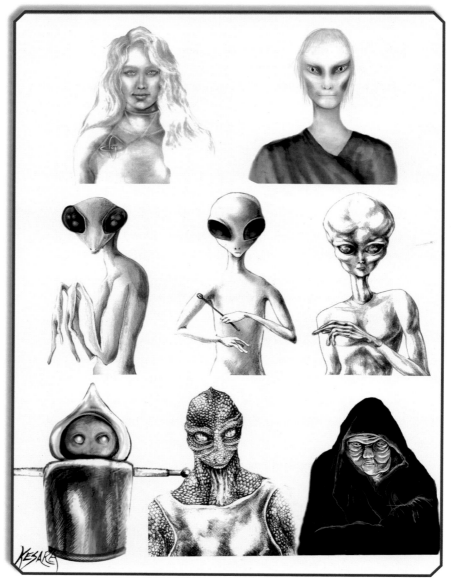

Figure 3.2 *Here are some of the most commonly reported types of E.T.s. Upper row from left to right: Pleiadian/Nordic, Tall Humanoid; Second row from left to right: Praying Mantis, Short Gray, Tall Gray; Bottom row from left to right: Robotic, Reptilion/Reptoid, Dwarf/Short Humanoid.* (Kesara Art)

Because of the physical evidence, Zamora's case generated huge interest. Further research revealed several other witnesses who also saw the UFO as it darted away. Hector Quintanilla, who headed the Air Force investigation, wrote, "There is no doubt that Lonnie Zamora saw an object which left quite an impression on him . . . He is puzzled by what he saw, and frankly, so are we. This is the best documented case on record."

Investigators later discovered that the symbol on the side of the craft was the Arabic symbol for Venus. Could this have been the origin of the UFO craft? While astronomers have discovered that Venus is too hot to sustain life, perhaps the E.T.s have used their technology to build a base there. And in fact, E.T.s have claimed to have bases in various places on earth and other planets.[23]

THE FALCON LAKE UFO LANDING

One of Canada's most famous UFO landings occurred on May 20, 1967, with prospector Stephen Michalek bearing witness. On that day, he was in the wilderness near Falcon Lake, Manitoba in Canada when he saw two red glowing, cigar-shaped objects in the sky.

Suddenly, one of them swooped down and landed 160 feet away. Michalek could see it was about 35 feet in diameter. A door opened, and he could see strange colored lights flashing inside. He crept closer until he heard weird voices coming from inside. Thinking maybe it was an experimental Russian craft, he asked in Russian, "Do you speak Russian?" When he got no response, he tried five different languages. Still there was no response.

Michalek then decided to get closer. He walked right up to the craft and looked through the opening. He saw a bright "maze" of lights on a panel, all flashing in different sequences. Suddenly, the opening quickly closed and the craft took off straight up.

Michalek felt a blast of hot air and his shirt was set on fire. Almost immediately he started to feel very sick. He was rushed to the hospital where he began to suffer a number of alarming symptoms including a headache, diarrhea, weakness, dizziness, vomiting, hives, numbness, swelling of joints, eye irritation, and burns. He was unable to keep any food down and lost 22 pounds. His blood lymphocyte level decreased from a normal 25 percent to a dangerous 16 percent. More than 27 doctors examined Michalek, and the only explanation that seemed to fit was exposure to radiation. [24]

THE DELPHOS, KANSAS UFO LANDING

A significant portion of UFO encounters involve children and teenagers, perhaps because they spend a lot of time outdoors. On November 2, 1971, 16-year-old Ronald Johnson was doing chores in his backyard near Delphos, Kansas. Suddenly, he heard a loud rumbling sound. Turning around, he saw a giant muffin-shaped object covered with blue, red, and orange lights, resting on a beam of light about two feet off the ground and only 75 feet away. The object was about eight feet wide and glowed so bright, it hurt Ronald's eyes to look at it.

Ronald called for his parents. At that moment, the object quickly darted away, knocking over a tree and taking off up into the sky. Ronald's parents came out in time to see the strange object dart southwards across the sky. At the same time, two of the neighbors had also observed the object land and take off.

At this point, everyone noticed that the area where the UFO had hovered was glowing with a ring of eerie light. Mrs. Johnson touched the glow and her hand suddenly became numb. They called the police and asked them to investigate. Even the police were impressed by the strange landing trace evidence.

Leading scientists were given samples of the soil for chemical analysis. The soil turned out to have many unusual properties, including high levels of calcium, sodium, and other elements that shouldn't have been present. Also, the soil appeared to have been crystallized, and it would no longer become wet or hold water. Finally, the area of the ring refused to support life. For years, no plants would grow

Cases of High Strangeness

While stories of UFOs and aliens are strange enough, some cases have an extremely high strangeness level. These rare cases are so bizarre that even UFO investigators have trouble understanding or categorizing the encounter. What follows are three famous cases involving high strangeness.

On October 13, 1917, a crowd of 70,000 people in Fatima, Portugal, observed a fantastic aerial display involving a huge, disk-like object that cast down brilliant rays of colored light on the stunned onlookers. This sounds like a typical UFO, except that in this case, three young girls who claimed to be in communication with the Virgin Mary predicted the sighting. Was it a UFO encounter or a religious miracle?

In October of 1973, an intense UFO wave swept across Pennsylvania. The wave was typical, involving bright, silent disk-shaped crafts darting overhead, chasing cars, and landing. Again, this sounds like an average UFO encounter, except at the same time, Pennsylvania was also experiencing an intense wave of Bigfoot encounters. Says lead investigator Stan Gordon, "During the 1973 Pennsylvania outbreak . . . well-documented incidents occurred where both a UFO and Bigfoot were observed in the same place, at the same time, by more than one witness."

On September 3, 1965, a purple beam of light from a UFO struck policeman Robert Goode of Damon, Texas. Earlier, Goode had been bitten by a baby pet alligator and suffered a wound on his finger. After the UFO encounter, he took off the bandage and the wound had disappeared. There are now more than 150 cases of UFO healings on record. For more information on these and other high-strangeness cases, check out the following books:

- *Dimensions: A Casebook of Alien Contact* by Jacques Vallee.
- *The Mysterious Valley* by Christopher O'Brien.
- *The Unidentified* by Jerome Clark and Loren Coleman.

where the UFO had hovered. Today, the case is considered a classic "landing trace" case.[25]

THE UFO LANDING IN VORONEZH, RUSSIA

Starting in late September 1989, the city of Voronezh, Russia, experienced a wave of sightings involving many UFOs of different shapes and sizes. Then, on the afternoon of September 27, 1989, several children were playing soccer in a local park when a giant red sphere, 30 feet in diameter, landed right next to them. A huge crowd quickly gathered. Suddenly, a hatch opened in the craft and two creatures stepped out. One was a short robotic-looking figure. The other was an estimated 10 feet tall! The alien appeared to have "three eyes," was wearing a silver jumpsuit, bronze-colored boots, and a round disk on his chest.

The crowd began to panic when the 10-foot-tall alien pointed a long tube at one of the witnesses, who reportedly disappeared and reappeared seconds later. Immediately afterward, the aliens stepped back into the sphere, which took off straight up.

Because there were so many witnesses, and because of the earlier wave of sightings, the event caused a huge sensation. The news agency TASS picked up the story, and before long, it was front-page news across the world.

The landing was investigated by a wide variety of scientists including medical investigators, psychologists, criminologists, and more. It was discovered that numerous other people in the area had seen and even photographed the UFOs. Some of the witnesses suffered weird side effects such as insomnia. Others reported **electromagnetic effects** on their TVs and appliances. Most exciting, however, was the analysis of the landing site. Depressions in the ground showed that the object weighed several tons. Radiation was found in the soil, as were unusually high levels of certain elements—in particular, phosphorus. The Voronezh landing remains one of the most famous UFO landings in Russian history, and as of yet, it is still unexplained.[26]

Figure 3.3 *On September 27, 1989, a group of children were playing soccer in a field in Voronezh, Russia when a giant sphere-shaped UFO landed and ejected several creatures, including one very tall E.T. The encounter took place during a local wave of sightings.* (Kesara Art)

UFO landings are distributed throughout the entire world and involve a huge variety of beings, including robots, humanoids, gray-type E.T.s, and many more. The fact that E.T.s are so varied has puzzled researchers, as does the fact that E.T.s look even remotely like human beings. Could it be that humans and E.T.s are related somehow? As it turns out, some UFO abductees (people taken onboard UFOs) have been told by the aliens that humans are, in fact, genetically related to E.T.s. In the next chapter, we shall examine the closest of all types of encounters: cases in which people claim to have been taken onboard a UFO.

Taken Onboard

On March 22, 1953, Sara Shaw and Jan Whitley were asleep in their cabin in a remote location in Tujunga Canyon, California. It was around 2:00 a.m., when they both woke up to find the interior of the cabin illuminated by a bright, eerie blue light. They jumped up to investigate, and then suddenly lost consciousness. When they woke up, two hours had passed and the strange light was gone. Knowing something very strange had happened to them, they fled the cabin in a panic.

Unfortunately, at the time, UFO abductions were unheard of. Not knowing what happened, or whom to tell, the witnesses kept the event a secret for more than 20 years. Then in 1975, after several other similar cases had surfaced, they went under **hypnosis** to investigate the two hours of **missing time**. To their shock, they remembered being struck by a beam of light and floated onboard a UFO that had landed outside their cabin. Under hypnosis, Sara Shaw described her experience: "I'm on the beam of light. I'm standing on it and it's angled . . . it's about the same angle as an escalator would be, except it doesn't have ridges or steps. It's just a very smooth, solid beam, and you just kind of stand in it."

Shaw described one of the entities as being "not ugly to look at, or funny-looking, but they're kind of funny in a way . . . his head is elongated. It's like an egg, but one that isn't really wider at the top or the bottom." She noticed that the entities were basically humanoid—tall and thin with large hairless heads. Said Sara, "If there's any hair, it's underneath this skin-tight–it's like a ski mask, but it's almost a part of the skin."

Once inside, the ladies were amazed by the enormous size of the craft. Said Shaw, "The inside of the ship is like one giant room, and there's a second level above us. It has circular balconies . . . the balcony goes all the way around the entire inside."

The craft was very clean and brightly lit. The entities didn't speak but communicated telepathically. The witnesses were taken to separate rooms, laid out on tables, and given a thorough medical examination. The E.T.s seemed particularly interested in an old surgical scar on Jan Whitley's body. They told the women not to be afraid, that they wouldn't hurt them. The E.T.s said that they had the ability to cure cancer, and that finally, they would meet again.

Afterwards, the ladies were returned to their cabin with no conscious memory of the event. Later on, both would experience further abductions, which spread like a contagion among their close friends. The case shocked the UFO community. At that point in time, only a few other cases were known. The idea that people could go inside UFOs was shocking, even to UFO investigators, and the idea that abductees would not even remember the experience was unthinkable. However, it wouldn't be long before more cases would occur.[27]

By far the strangest aspect of UFOs are close encounters of the fourth kind, or cases in which people claim to have been taken onboard an alien craft. There are now thousands of such recorded cases, often called UFO abductions. The UFO abduction phenomenon has been studied extensively. In 1987, folklorist Thomas Bullard analyzed 309 cases and came up with the basic model of a UFO abduction. According to Bullard, there are seven main events that occur, including:

1   Capture

2   Examination

3   Conference

Of course, this is only a rough pattern. The truth is, each encounter is as individual as the people who have them. In some cases, people are only able to remember their encounter with the aid of hypnosis. In other cases, hypnosis is not necessary.

It's important to remember that the UFO phenomenon is still a mystery. While the main theory is that UFO occupants are extraterrestrials from other planets, that is not the only theory. Some UFO investigators believe that UFOs are interdimensional rather than extraterrestrial. They point out that UFOs can move at right angles and appear or disappear out of thin air. It is also possible that UFOs come not from outer space, but from the inner-earth, and that they, like humans, have evolved on this planet. Some abductees have even been told by the E.T.s that they are actually time travelers from the future. Any of these theories could be true. The best way to determine which theory fits best is to examine the cases themselves.

THE ABDUCTION OF ANTONIO VILLAS BOAS

The first abduction to be publicly revealed occurred in a remote area of Saõ Paolo, Brazil. On October 5, 1957, young farmer Antonio Villas Boas and his brother both observed a strange glowing object hovering over their farm. The next night, the UFO returned. This time, it hovered directly over their home, lighting up the inside like daylight.

Then, on October 7, 1957, Antonio was plowing the fields very late, at around 1:00 a.m., when the UFO appeared again. This time, the object hovered over the tractor, and then landed in the field. Antonio could then see that it was a "strange type of machine." It was large, egg-shaped, covered with colored lights and stood on three metal legs. Antonio tried to drive away, but suddenly his tractor engine died. Antonio then jumped out of the tractor and tried to run away. Suddenly, he was surrounded by several short figures dressed in tight-fitting gray jumpsuits and dark helmets. They quickly grabbed Antonio and pulled him aboard the craft.

Antonio found himself inside a small room with polished metal walls and bright lights. He was taken into another larger room where the E.T.s began to talk to each other in a strange "grunting" language. The figures rubbed a strange lotion on Antonio's skin, and took a blood sample with a strange instrument. He was then placed in another room and made to breathe a strange gas mixture. Finally, he met with a female E.T. who seemed physically attracted to him. Antonio fought off her advances as best as he could. Afterwards, he was led out of the room and taken on a short tour of the craft. He was shown the engine room, which he was unable to understand. He attempted to take a piece of machinery to use as proof of his experience, but the E.T.s took it away. He was then escorted out of the craft. Seconds later, the UFO took off, never to return.

In the aftermath, Antonio suffered a number of physical symptoms including insomnia, extreme thirst, loss of appetite, vomiting, eye irritation, and a strange rash. He also had a minor puncture wound where the E.T.s had taken a blood sample. The case was reported to a local doctor, who contacted UFO investigators. And so the world's first actual UFO abduction case came to light, but because it was so bizarre and totally unique, it was largely ignored by the public. Four years later, however, an event would occur that would change the way people felt about UFOs forever.[28]

THE ABDUCTION OF BETTY AND BARNEY HILL

On September 19, 1961, post-office employee Barney Hill and his wife, Betty (a social worker) drove home late at night through the

The 10 Signs of a UFO Abduction

Onboard UFO encounters are sometimes shrouded in amnesia. For this reason, many people may have experienced a UFO abduction and not even know it. What follows are the top 10 indications that someone may have been abducted by aliens:

1   Close-up UFO encounter(s) (within about 1,000 feet or closer)

2   Missing time (a period of time that you cannot remember, a blackout)

3   Seeing figures/apparitions in home (usually in bedroom at night)

4   UFO dreams (usually of being onboard a craft)

5   Strong emotional reaction to UFOs (either attraction or revulsion)

6   Unexplained scars (witness is unable to say where the scars originated)

7   Unexplained healing or injury (unable to say where originated)

8   Phobia of clowns or dwarfs (this is present in many UFO abductees)

9   Poltergeist-like activity (abductees experience many paranormal events)

10 History of UFOs in family (other family members have encounters)

White Mountains of New Hampshire. Suddenly, Betty noticed an unusually bright star-like object pacing their car. The couple watched and theorized that it was perhaps a satellite or even a plane. Then the object came closer. Through binoculars, Betty could see a row of windows and colored lights. Barney stopped the car, looked through the binoculars, and saw that his wife was right: It was an object. He also saw the row of windows, and saw that, inside, there were several short figures dressed in strange uniforms.

He dashed back into the car and told his wife that they were about to be "captured." The fearful couple took off down the road. Suddenly, they both heard an odd beeping noise and started to feel strange. The next thing they knew, two hours had passed and they were approaching their hometown. Something had happened, but neither could remember what.

Over the next few weeks, Betty began to have dreams that she had been taken onboard and examined. Meanwhile, Barney began suffering health problems, including a rash, an ulcer, and anxiety attacks. Finally, they sought the help of a doctor who recommended hypnosis.

Under hypnosis, the couple recalled seeing the UFO, hearing the beeping noise, and then coming upon a "road block." The craft had landed in the center of the road. Their car was surrounded by short figures with large, hairless heads and dark, almond-shaped eyes. They were both taken onboard and separated into different examination rooms. They were told to have no fear, that the E.T.s meant no harm, and that they would be returned shortly. Both were then undressed and given a full medical examination. The E.T.s took skin scrapings, saliva samples, blood samples, locks of hair, and nail clippings. They seemed particularly fascinated by Barney's false teeth, and couldn't understand why Betty's teeth couldn't also be removed.

After the examination, Betty was shown a book with various strange symbols. She asked where they came from, and she was shown a holographic star map. Afterwards, Betty and Barney were returned to their car and told they wouldn't remember anything. Although they didn't recall the incident at first, there were several clues that something strange had happened. Not only was there missing time, but their dog Delsie was scared and cowering in the back seat. Betty's dress had a strange stain on it. And the car hood had several weird, polished spots on it. When they held up a compass to the spots, the needle would spin.

After later recalling the entire story while under hypnosis, their case became the first widely publicized UFO abduction. To this day, nobody has been able to dispute the case.

Figure 4.1 *Barney and Betty Hill, who claim to have been abducted by aliens, describe their experience as Barney holds up a drawing of a UFO. The Hills were the first people to go public claiming to have been abducted inside a UFO.* (Bettmann/Corbis)

Most amazing is the star map. Years later, schoolteacher Marjorie Fish analyzed the star map that Betty had seen aboard the craft and drawn under hypnosis. Using new astronomy charts, Fish was able to determine that the E.T.s home star was Zeta-Reticuli. Today, the case is considered a classic and has been the subject of a book and a television movie.[29]

By this time, researchers had uncovered numerous other cases involving the strange feature of "missing time." While missing time is now a recognized symptom of a close encounter, the first cases baffled investigators. Today, most researchers believe that the amnesia is placed upon abductees by the aliens to either protect the aliens' activities from becoming known, or to protect the abductees from potentially traumatic memories. In either case, many abductees suffer from this bizarre memory loss in association with their close encounters. Researchers have helped people overcome this memory block through the use of regressive hypnosis. Usually used on victims of trauma such as child abuse or war victims, hypnosis allows the patient to mentally relax enough to access memories that are normally kept hidden from the conscious mind. Some skeptics claim that hypnosis can lead to "false memory syndrome," or, in other words, imagining events that didn't happen. Most of today's leading abduction researchers, however, support hypnosis as a valid tool to recover hidden abduction memories.

THE HICKSON-PARKER ABDUCTION

One of the most electrifying UFO contact cases occurred on October 11, 1973, to two fishermen in Pascagoula, Mississippi. On that evening, Charles Hickson and his friend Calvin Parker sat in their favorite fishing spot near an old shipyard. Hickson had just caught a fish when they both heard a weird "zipping sound" coming from behind and above. Turning around, they saw a 30-foot-long football-shaped object with two portholes landing 60 feet away. Suddenly, a door opened and a bright white light streamed out. Seconds later, three five-foot-tall figures glided out of the craft and floated toward the two frightened fishermen.

It was instantly obvious that these figures were not human. Says Hickson, "If they had a more human likeness, it would not have shocked me so. The head seemed to come directly to the shoulders, no neck, and something resembling a nose came out to a point about two inches long. On each side of the head, about where ears would be, was something similar to the nose. Directly under the nose was a slit resembling a mouth. The arms were something like human arms, but long in proportion to the body; the hands resembled a mitten—there was a thumb attached. The legs remained together and the feet looked something like elephant's feet. The entire body was wrinkled and had a grayish color. There could have been eyes, but the area above the nose was so wrinkled, I couldn't tell."

Both the men had the impression that the figures were actually robots. They had no time to run before the aliens surrounded them and pulled them onboard the craft. They were each taken to separate rooms. Calvin Parker was so frightened that he fainted. Charles Hickson, however, had been in the Korean War and knew what intense fear was like. This experience, he said, was far scarier. He found himself in a room with white, rounded walls, floating and unable to move. Next, a bright light with an eye-shaped lens came out of the wall and circled around his body as if it was examining him. The E.T.s left for a moment. Hickson called out for his friend, but got no response. Moments later, the E.T.s returned and floated Hickson back into the first room and then outside the craft. Calvin was also there, shaking with fear. The E.T.s then returned to their craft and took off. As they left, Hickson received a strong message through **telepathy** from the E.T.s: "We are peaceful; we meant you no harm."

The two men raced to the police station to report their encounter. To see if they were lying, the sheriff hid a tape recorder inside his desk and left the men alone. He knew that if they were lying, they would probably talk about it. But when he reviewed the tape, the men stuck to their story. Parker even broke down crying. Further investigation revealed that several police officers in the area had also seen UFOs around the same time. The case soon became hugely famous. Both men later underwent hypnosis and lie detector tests. No evidence of hoaxing was ever found. Hickson later had further encounters involving much of his family. [30]

THE ABDUCTION OF SERGEANT CHARLES MOODY

Even policemen can be abducted by UFOs. At about 1:00 a.m., on the evening of August 13, 1975, Sergeant Charles Moody of Alamogordo, New Mexico, drove out into the desert to watch a meteor shower that was due to occur. However, he got much more than he bargained for. As he was watching for shooting stars, a 50-foot-long metallic, saucer-shaped craft landed next to him. Frightened, Sergeant Moody jumped into his car and attempted to drive away. But for some strange reason, his car would not start. Then, his entire body became numb. Just when his fear increased, the object suddenly took off.

Moody raced home to tell his wife. He was shocked to find it was already 3:00 a.m., and that two hours had passed. Had he been taken onboard? At first he didn't remember, but over the next few days and weeks, he spontaneously recalled everything that had happened.

He remembered that he was, in fact, taken onboard. He was sitting in his car when the numbness came over his body. Next, several "beings" exited the craft. Says Moody, "The beings were about five feet tall and very much like us except their heads were larger and hairless, their ears were very small, eyes a little larger than ours, nose small and the mouth had very thin lips. I would say their weight was maybe between 110–130 pounds. They have speech, but their lips did not move. Their type of clothing was skintight. I could not see any zippers or buttons at all. The color of their clothes was black except for one of them who had a silver-white looking suit on."

Moody was taken into a very clean room with white, rounded walls and indirect lighting. One of the beings examined him and told him, "I will not hurt you. We are not meant to hurt you." Moody asked if he could see the engine room. They agreed and took him to a lower level. He saw a complex machine involving long metallic rods and large, crystal-like spheres.

The E.T.s explained that the ship operated using the principle of positive and negative magnetic poles. They told him that they had a much larger mother ship, and that there were many other races of E.T.s who were also observing and studying the planet. They warned him against the use of nuclear weapons. They also said that they had a plan of limited contact and would one day reveal their existence publicly to the world. Finally, he was told that it was time for him to go and that he wouldn't remember what happened until a few days afterwards. Moody was then placed back in his car, where he watched the UFO take off.

After remembering the onboard part of his experience, Moody realized how important his story was, and he contacted local UFO investigators. A thorough investigation revealed no inconsistencies in his account. Today, Moody's case remains undisputed. He is only one of several policemen who claim to have been abducted by aliens.[31]

THE ABDUCTION OF TRAVIS WALTON

Probably the most famous UFO abduction case of all occurred on November 5, 1975, to a forestry worker named Travis Walton. On that day, Walton and six other woodcutters were clearing old growth in a forest near Snowflake, Arizona. At the end of the day, they drove home along a remote dirt road. Suddenly, all six men observed an extremely bright light shining through the trees. As they got closer, they could see it was actually a huge, metallic, saucer-shaped craft, glowing with an eerie light.

Travis Walton had always been interested in UFOs and without thinking, he ran out of the car and underneath the craft. Moments later, a beam of light shot out of the craft and hit Travis in the chest, knocking him unconscious. Thinking they were all about to be abducted, the other men drove off in a panic.

Meanwhile, Travis woke up to find that he was lying on a table in a small, round room. At first, he thought he was in a hospital room. Then, he saw the creatures: several five-foot-tall figures dressed in orange jumpsuits. Each had a large, hairless head and large dark eyes. Says Travis, "Their smooth skin was so pale that it looked chalky . . . their overall look was disturbingly like that of a human fetus."

Walton suddenly realized that he wasn't inside any hospital: He was inside the UFO. He jumped up and grabbed a glass-like rod and raised it to protect himself. The E.T.s filed out of the room. Travis then crept outside into a curving hallway, and then into the next room, where he found a strange chair with unusual-looking knobs and switches on the armrest. He sat down in the chair and was shocked to see the walls suddenly become transparent. All around him he could see bright stars glittering in the deep blackness of space. He started to fiddle with the knobs, but decided he had better not.

At that moment, a tall human-looking figure with blond hair, tan skin, and a tight-fitting jumpsuit appeared and grabbed Travis by the arm, pulling him into another room. Travis asked him all kinds of questions, but the man refused to answer. Travis was taken into a room like a large aircraft hangar, where he saw several other UFO craft. Next, they took him into a small room, placed him on a table, and put a mask over his face. Walton instantly lost consciousness.

He woke up lying alongside a highway several miles away. The UFO took off straight up and disappeared. Travis went to the nearest phone booth and called for home. That's when he got another huge shock. He had been missing for five days! Not only that, but his fellow employees were all suspects in a police investigation for having murdered Travis. Although the men had insisted from the beginning that Travis was abducted by a UFO, nobody believed them. Now that Travis was found alive, his UFO story became an instant media sensation. All of the men underwent a polygraph examination. Everyone passed except for one, who was too emotionally upset to take an accurate test.

Years later, the event was made into the Hollywood blockbuster, *Fire in the Sky*. Many skeptics have attacked the case, saying that the story was made up and Walton could have hidden in the wilderness for the five days he was missing. However, no evidence of this was ever found and the case has never been disproved. [32]

THE SMITH-THOMAS-STAFFORD ABDUCTION

Some skeptics have argued that people who think they were abducted by aliens were just imagining things. However, this theory does not account for multiple-witness cases, such as what happened to three ladies from Liberty, Kentucky. On the evening of January 20, 1976, Mona Stafford, Louise Smith, and Elaine Thomas were driving home after dining out when they saw a "fiery red" object swoop down from the sky. At first, they thought it was a crashing airplane, but then the object stopped and hovered above them. At this point, they could see that it was a large, disk-shaped craft, with a row of red lights flashing around the circumference.

The disk quickly circled around behind their car, and then several things happened at once. The car began to speed along at 80 miles per hour, though Louise Smith, who was driving, had removed her foot from the gas pedal. At the same time, a bluish light filled the car, which began to shake and float and was then pulled backwards. The car then stalled and, as it was lifted into the air, all three felt a burning sensation and then blacked out. In what seemed like only a few seconds later, they found themselves eight miles further ahead on the road, still in their car. They realized immediately that they were missing more than an hour of time and that something very strange had happened that they couldn't remember.

Afterwards, they suffered from a number of alarming symptoms, including headaches, eye irritation, first-degree burns on their necks, fatigue, weight loss, nausea, vomiting, and diarrhea. Investigators were called in who later put the ladies under hypnosis. Each of them recalled being taken onboard the craft. The interior of the craft was white, blue, and dark green and had three separate levels. There were strange control panels with colored lights. The ladies were separated into different rooms and examined by short humanoids dressed in white uniforms that covered everything except the eyes. Elaine Thomas felt that the E.T.s were particularly interested in learning about her "intellectual and emotional processes." Mona Stafford was told that the E.T.s were testing them to see if they could withstand the gravitational forces of interstellar travel. They told Smith that their own home world was dying and that they were gathering information to see if the E.T.s could survive in the Earth's atmosphere. They also said that they had the ability to control weather patterns.

Afterwards, the witnesses were traumatized not only emotionally, but also physically. Because of their physical symptoms, their case gained considerable attention. All three were given lie detector tests, which they passed. Stafford also noticed that her watch was running at twice its normal speed immediately after the abduction. There was other physical evidence: The taillights and brake lights on the car were broken and the paint on the hood was blistered and peeling. Investigators later located other witnesses in the area who observed what appeared to be the same UFO that abducted the three ladies, making the case one of the best-verified on record.[33]

Alien Implants

*O*ne of the most bizarre and controversial aspects of UFO abductions is the possibility that many people may have had **alien implants** put into their bodies by aliens. This first came to the attention of researchers when abductees reported being taken aboard UFOs, examined by E.T.s, and pierced by large needles that had small, BB-sized/shaped objects on their ends. Several abductees have gone to medical doctors and obtained X-rays and magnetic resonance images (MRIs) that show the presence of these "foreign bodies." Most of these objects are found in the arms, legs, and heads of abductees.

The purpose of these implants is not known, but theories include tracking, mind-control, monitoring the health of the body, or measuring pollution levels. Today, researchers have made great strides forward in this area. More than a dozen of these alien implants have been removed by doctors and studied in scientific laboratories. The results are nothing less than astonishing:

1　Several of the implants emit a strong electromagnetic field.

2　There is no foreign-body reaction in surrounding human tissue.

3　The identical cantaloupe seed-like implant appears in many cases.

4　The implants are metallic, made with iron usually found only in meteorites.

5　The implants are fluorescent and glow pink or green under ultraviolet light.

6　The objects appear to be artificially constructed, not naturally occurring.

(continues)

(continued)

Many other unusual properties are still being uncovered. Research into alien implants is currently being continued by researchers such as Dr. Roger Leir, DPM (Doctor of Podiatric Medicine), author of *The Aliens and the Scalpel*, a leading book about alien implants. Some researchers feel that alien implant cases represent the best proof for UFOs to date. Skeptics, however, have pointed out that no alien implant has ever been found to contain unknown elements that cannot be found on earth, nor is there any proof that they are, in fact, extraterrestrial.

THE ABDUCTIONS OF WHITLEY STRIEBER

In 1988, popular fiction novelist Whitley Strieber stunned the world with the publication of his non-fiction book *Communion: A True Story*, about his repeated encounters with alien beings in his cabin in upstate New York. The whole ordeal began on October 4, 1985. On that evening, Strieber and his wife had invited friends over to stay in their cabin. Sometime in the middle of the night, everybody woke up to find the cabin flooded with an intense, white light. They also heard strange noises, as if there were other people in the house. Nobody, however, could explain these strange events, and so they were largely ignored.

Then, on December 25, 1985, Strieber woke up to find a strange creature entering his bedroom. It was about four feet tall, dressed in a strange uniform and helmet, and carrying a strange wand in its hand. Strieber just had time to sit up when the figure rushed into his bedroom and zapped him on the forehead with the wand. The next thing he remembered, several gray-type E.T.s rushed into the room, picked him up, and floated him out of his cabin and into his backyard. Next, he was sucked up into a UFO. He was undressed and underwent a quick medical examination.

Strieber was understandably terrified and began screaming. The E.T.s seemed puzzled by his fear and asked him, "What can we do to make you stop screaming?" Strieber said, "You can let me smell you." He wasn't sure why he made this bizarre request, except that perhaps it would help ground him in reality and calm him down.

The E.T. agreed and Strieber smelled the creature, which had an odor of cinnamon and wet cardboard. Somehow, the technique worked and Strieber calmed down. He was then dressed and returned back to his cabin.

This, however, was only the tip of the iceberg. Strieber explored his memories under hypnosis and learned that he had been having encounters all his life, and they were still going on. At first, he thought he was mentally ill, so he went to a psychologist; however, the psychological tests showed that he was psychologically healthy. He went to a medical doctor and discovered that he had unknown "foreign bodies" implanted in his brain. Strieber believes the objects may be "alien implants." Several people, in fact, have reported similar objects in their bodies, which they found using X-rays and magnetic resonance imaging (MRIs).

Strieber's case involves literally dozens of supporting witnesses, making it one of the best verified on record. To this day, Strieber continues to have encounters.[34]

Onboard UFO encounters tend to follow the same pattern as outlined by Thomas Bullard, with the most common onboard experience being a physical examination. However, why so many people are being abducted remains a mystery. The good news is that it doesn't appear that the aliens are evil or bent on taking over the world. However, neither does it appear that they are here to help. Instead, most researchers feel that the aliens are probably more like scientists or even tourists. In other words, UFOs may show a deep interest in humanity, but, for the most part, they stay out of human affairs.

UFO Crashes

It was the morning of April 19, 1897, when 10-year-old Charlie Stephens and his father were shocked to observe a large, metallic, cigar-shaped object with bright lights passing overhead at a low elevation. The unidentified craft flew to the north, heading toward the town of Aurora, Texas. Suddenly, Charlie and his father heard a huge explosion and saw a bright flame. At the same time, numerous other citizens in town were also watching the object, and saw it crash into a local windmill and explode. The craft was destroyed and the sole occupant was killed. The townspeople gathered and witnessed the wreckage of the weird craft and the body of the airship pilot. The apparent alien was given a proper burial at the local cemetery. While this story may sound unusual, it is actually the world's first known UFO crash. At the time, the United States was in the middle of a wave of sightings involving hundreds of these mysterious craft. The Aurora UFO crash, however, is the only known case of a crashed airship.

It may seem surprising that something so advanced as an interplanetary vehicle could crash. However, if UFOs are truly physical spacecraft from other planets, then it should also be possible that they might malfunction or even crash. While UFOs appear to be technologically superior to our own aircraft, apparently sometimes things go wrong. Reports of UFO crashes are extremely rare, but investigators have currently gathered more than 50 separate cases. Unfortunately, most of these cases are short on evidence; there are lots of stories, but very little hard proof.

A few cases have risen above the rest in credibility, however. In these cases, there seems to be little doubt that something crashed and was allegedly recovered by secret military forces. The question is: What was it?

THE ROSWELL UFO CRASH

This much is fact: On July 4, 1947, *something* fell to the earth and crashed on a remote ranch outside of Roswell, New Mexico. It was quickly recovered by the United States Army Air Force and shipped off to Wright-Patterson Air Force Base in Ohio. Events actually began earlier that week when radar operators in Roswell detected strange images darting at high speeds across their radarscopes. Then on July 4, a severe thunderstorm struck Roswell. The next day, rancher Mac Brazel found a large amount of "strange debris" on his ranch. At the same time, a group of archaeologists stumbled upon a metallic disk that had crashed into the hillside. It was cracked open and four or five gray-type E.T.s were lying inside and outside the craft, with two apparently still alive. The military converged upon the scene and quickly carted everything away.

The next day, the military released a statement to the press saying that they had recovered a "flying disk." This incredible announcement shocked the world. The following day, however, the military released another statement: They had made a mistake. It wasn't a crashed UFO; it was only a "weather balloon."

The media accepted the new explanation, and the entire story faded away. For more than 20 years, all the witnesses involved in the Roswell incident said nothing. Then, in the early 1970s, Major Jesse Marcel decided he could no longer remain silent.

Major Marcel was an Army Intelligence officer at Roswell, and was one of the first people to visit the crash site and handle the wreckage.

What to Do If You See a UFO

How do you know if you are seeing a true UFO? And what should you do if you do see one? The following three steps will help guide you in the event of your very own close encounter:

STEP ONE: CRITICAL OBSERVATION.

If you see something you think might be a UFO, you will first want to determine if it might be something conventional, such as an airplane, ball lightning, or something else mundane. UFOs usually display three main characteristics: strange sound, strange appearance, and strange movement. If what you are observing looks strange, sounds strange, and moves strangely, you may be seeing an actual UFO. For example, a plane displays red and green wing lights, has a loud engine noise, and usually moves in a straight line. UFOs, however, are often quiet or silent, are covered with multi-colored lights, and hover or dart at right angles.

STEP TWO: CONFIRMATION.

Once you have determined that you are seeing a genuine UFO, you will want to try to confirm this fact. One good way is to get more witnesses. A UFO sighting by one person is easily ignored, but if a dozen or more people see a UFO, the encounter can become front-page news and make UFO history. Another method of confirmation is to obtain a photograph of the object. The old saying "A picture is worth a thousand words" is especially true with UFOs.

STEP THREE: REPORT ENCOUNTER.

Following your encounter, you should file an official report of the sighting. You can call the local police or report your sighting to the

(continues)

(continued)

Mutual UFO Network (**MUFON**) or the National UFO Reporting Service (NUFORC). (See the "Further Research" section at the end of this book.) By reporting your case, you may discover that there are other witnesses to your encounter, that the area has a history of UFO sightings, or that there is a conventional explanation. Most importantly, recording your encounter will be one step closer to solving the UFO mystery.

Marcel now said that the object was *not* a weather balloon, but an actual alien craft. Says Marcel, "It was something I had never seen before, or since, for that matter. I didn't know what it was, but it certainly wasn't anything built by us and it most certainly wasn't any weather balloon."

After Major Marcel, several other witnesses stepped forward and told about their involvement. It soon became clear why there had been no talk about the incident for so many years. Many of the witnesses claimed that they had been "threatened" by Air Force officers to remain silent.

Mac Brazel, the rancher who first found the wreckage, refused to speak about the incident, but did say that, "I am sure what I found was not any weather observation balloon."

Brazel's son, Bill, later spoke publicly. He also handled some of the wreckage, and said, "There were several different types of stuff. Of course, all I had was small bits and pieces, but one thing that I can say about it was that it was sure light in weight. It weighed almost nothing . . . there were also several bits of a metal-like substance, something on the order of tinfoil, except this stuff wouldn't tear."

Amateur archaeologist Barney Barnett was collecting stones on the day the Roswell crash occurred, and he claims to have been on the scene of the actual crash site. He says, "I realized it wasn't a plane at all, but some sort of metallic, disc-shaped object about 25 or 30 feet across . . . It was not all that big. It seemed to be made of metal that looked like dirty stainless steel. The machine had been split open by explosion or impact. I tried to get close to see what the bodies were like . . . They were like humans, but they were not humans. The heads

Figure 5.1 *The United States Air Force has consistently denied that a UFO crashed outside of Roswell, New Mexico. Here USAF officer Irving Newton poses for reporters with the alleged wreckage from Roswell, which, according to the Air Force, is actually from a weather balloon. Firsthand witnesses, however, claim that the real alien materials were covered up. The controversy continues today.* (Mary Evans Picture Library)

were round, the eyes were small, and they had no hair . . . Their clothing seemed to be one-piece and gray in color."

Glenn Dennis was a mortician at Roswell. He provided several child-sized coffins to the military, which he later realized were for the burial of the aliens. He also observed some of the Roswell wreckage and claimed to have spoken to a nurse who saw the actual alien bodies.

The X-Files Reveals the Truth about UFOs

Many popular movies and television series have featured UFOs. But just how true are these stories? Surprisingly, some of them are truer than audiences might think. One example is the film *Close Encounters of the Third Kind*, which was allegedly based on an actual incident of a UFO reportedly landing at Holloman Air Force Base in 1954. However, the program that has earned the strongest reputation for revealing the truth about UFOs is the popular TV show, *The X-Files*. Although the series was fictional, many of its plot lines were inspired by actual incidents.

This hour-long weekly series featured FBI agents Dana Scully and Fox Mulder as they are called to investigate the FBI's cases involving the unexplained and the paranormal. Another memorable character is the mysterious Cigarette Smoking Man, who gives the agents clues when they need them, or scares them off when they get too close to the truth.

Besides being an exciting, well-acted drama, the show has featured virtually every aspect of the UFO cover-up, including everything from UFO abductions to crashed UFOs. Creator Chris Carter said that the secret to the show is research. Most of the plot-lines are taken from actual accounts. This gives the show a realism that keeps the fans coming back for more. Although the show is now cancelled, it is available on DVD and still

Frankie Rowe was only a teenager when her father brought home a piece of the Roswell wreckage. Military officers allegedly later entered their home, recovered the wreckage, and threatened the entire family if they spoke to anyone about the incident.

This case seemed to be the smoking gun to prove aliens had crashed on our planet. Dozens of UFO researchers focused on the incident. Before long, the list of witnesses grew to 200 people. The public began

Figure 5.2 *Agents Fox Mulder and Dana Scully, played by David Duchovny and Gillian Anderson, from the hit series* The X-Files. (Getty Images)

appears as reruns on several popular networks, and probably will for a long time. The truth is out there!

to demand answers. In 1995, New Mexico Congressman Steven Schiff attempted unsuccessfully to obtain official records of the incident.

Meanwhile, the United States Air Force released another statement, saying that the object was actually a secret **Mogul balloon** (a conventional weather balloon with high-tech detection equipment) and that the reported alien bodies were only test dummies used in rocket tests. The answer, it seemed, was finally found. However, this explanation fell to pieces when UFO researchers uncovered the fact that test dummies were not used until the mid-1950s, which was long after the Roswell crash occurred.

And so the controversy continues. Today, more than 10 books have been written about the events at Roswell, with some claiming that there was more than one crash. One of the latest books, *The Day After Roswell*, written by Colonel Philip Corso, claims that the Roswell wreckage was used to help create some of today's advanced technology, including the integrated circuit, fiber optics, night-vision goggles, and more. Today, the Roswell crash remains the single most famous UFO incident of all time.[35]

THE KECKSBURG UFO CRASH

On December 9, 1965, thousands of people across Canada and the United States observed a bright green meteor flash across the sky. At first, that seemed the end of the story, and for most people it was. For the citizens of Kecksburg, Pennsylvania, however, the story had just begun.

On that night, dozens of people in Kecksburg watched the meteor apparently slow down, make a gradual turn, and crash in the forest just outside of town. Instantly, calls poured into the local police station reporting a crash. Some thought it was a meteor. Others, however, were sure that it was some type of aircraft.

Policemen, firemen, and concerned citizens converged on the scene. When they arrived, they saw an incredible sight. A few people who managed to get close to the crash site said that they observed a twelve-foot-tall, acorn-shaped object. The object was metallic and had a band of hieroglyphic-type writing around its circumference. It was also reportedly glowing. As dozens of people began to surround the area, the United States military suddenly arrived. They ordered everybody away from the crash site at gunpoint, and quickly cordoned off the area. The object was then allegedly lifted up by crane onto a large flatbed truck, covered with a large tarp, and driven out of Kecksburg.

As with Roswell, several of the firsthand witnesses claimed they were ordered or threatened by unnamed military officials not to speak about what they saw. And so, like Roswell, the events that occurred in Kecksburg remained hidden for years. Then, in the early 1980s, a few witnesses began to come forward. Investigators then began the long search for more firsthand witnesses.

It took a while, but eventually more than 50 people came forward with firsthand knowledge about the events. Jim Romanowski said he observed the crashed UFO before being forcefully removed from the scene by military officials. Kecksburg resident Bill Bulebush was also there and saw the object carted away by the military. Truck driver, "Myron X," told investigators that he not only saw the object, he also saw what appeared to be an alien body. Although it was covered with a sheet, he could tell it was about four to five feet tall. He could see a hand sticking out from underneath. The hand looked "lizard-like" and had only three fingers.

Another witness, "Joel X," also watched as the Army surrounded the object and actually opened a hatch. Inside he saw "two fingers and an unusually long arm." The witness is certain it was not human. Kecksburg resident Don Sebastian heard about the crash on the radio. He drove to the site but was stopped by a roadblock. Sneaking past the roadblock, he saw rows of soldiers marching through the field, searching the area. Many more witnesses reported similar stories. Clearly, something unusual crashed outside of Kecksburg.

Figure 5.3 *On December 9, 1965, a mysterious object fell out of the sky and crashed into a forest outside of Kecksburg, Pennsylvania. Theories include a meteor, a Russian satellite, an experimental military aircraft, and of course, a UFO. Whatever it was, it was quickly recovered by the military.* (Kesara Art)

The public demanded answers. The meteor theory had already fallen apart because the speed of the object was much too slow, and several witnesses saw it turn in mid-flight. The military explained their presence in Kecksburg by saying they were recovering a Russian satellite. However, research showed that the satellite had actually fallen to earth more than 13 hours earlier.

The controversy continued in 2002 when the Sci-Fi Channel funded a new investigation, locating the actual crash site and bringing several more witnesses to light. In May 2003, researchers used the Freedom of Information Act to force NASA to release any documents they might have about the incident. As of 2006, the lawsuit against NASA remains unresolved. Today, research into the incident continues.[36]

THE SHAG HARBOR UFO CRASH

While the Roswell and Kecksburg incidents are the two most famous UFO crashes, the events that occurred in October 1967, at Shag Harbor, Canada, are even more impressive and have actually been partially confirmed through authentic government documents.

On October 4, Laurie Wickens and four other people were driving through the small fishing village of Shag Harbor in Nova Scotia when they saw a cluster of very bright lights swoop down out of the sky and crash into the nearby harbor. They drove quickly to the impact site and saw a strange 60-foot-long unidentified object slowly begin to sink beneath the surface. At the same time, local resident Mary Banks saw what she thought was an airplane crash into the harbor. Both Banks and Wickens called the authorities. At the same time, dozens of other calls flooded into local radio stations and newspaper offices.

Before long, a crowd of more than a dozen onlookers surrounded the beach area and watched the strange dark object several hundred yards offshore. At this point, the object sank beneath the surface, making the water bubble and froth. Several local fishermen offered their boats to search for the object. Six fishing boats criss-crossed the area, but were unable to locate the object. All they found was strange foam.

The Royal Canadian Coast Guard and the Royal Canadian Mounted Police were called to the scene. By the next morning, more than seven divers plunged into the bay to search for the object. At this point, many people still believed the object might be a plane, but all this was about to change. First of all, no planes were reported missing. Royal Canadian Air Force (RCAF) squadron leader William Bain served as spokesman for the RCAF and, in an official announcement, told the press that bright lights had been seen crashing into the harbor and that there was a strong possibility that "something concrete" may be found.

Then suddenly, the story ended. The Navy divers refused to talk to the press and the whole matter seemed forgotten. However, years later, several witnesses surfaced who said that the object was, in fact, a crashed UFO. Researchers Chris Styles and John Ledger joined forces and were able to obtain numerous testimonies from citizens and military personnel. Most witnesses insisted on being anonymous, but the stories they told were very similar.

Apparently, a very large object had, in fact, fallen into the harbor. It was first tracked on radar, and it was seen by more than 50 witnesses, including pilots and Coast Guard personnel. Divers on the scene located the object but were unable to identify it. The submerged object then moved north up the coast, where it was joined by another similar unidentified object. An apparent repair operation took place, which was observed and photographed by military personnel. The operation took six days, after which the UFOs suddenly raised up out of the ocean and took off into outer space. The Shag Harbor UFO, it seems, was only damaged, not destroyed. In either case, the UFO got away, and along with its disappearance went any solid conclusions about the mystery. Incredibly, however, researchers were able to obtain official government documents that state that an "unknown object" did in fact crash into Shag Harbor.[37]

UFO or USO?

UFO means "Unidentified Flying Object." But what if the UFO isn't flying in the air, and is, instead, underwater? In these cases, the objects are called USOs or "Unidentified Submarine Objects." USOs have been reported in all of the Earth's seven oceans and in many lakes and rivers. One very active area is off the coast of Southern California. Some UFO investigators believe that this might be the location of an underwater UFO base. What follows are four of the more than 50 encounters that have been reported in this area.

August 8, 1954

The crew of the Japanese steamship *Aliki* observe what they think is a fireball descending from the sky and plunging into the Pacific Ocean off the California coast. Moments later, the object reemerges from the ocean and then plunges back in. The crew notes the event in the ship's logbook.

January 15, 1956

Residents, security guards, lifeguards, and police officers observe a large, glowing object glide out of the sky and float about 75 yards offshore of Redondo Beach, California. After a few minutes the craft sinks beneath the waves and disappears.

February 5, 1964

Eleven survivors are rescued by the Coast Guard from their raft after the sinking of their yacht, the *Hattie D.*, off the California coast. The survivors claim that an unidentified submarine object rammed their boat, sinking it in a matter of minutes.

(continues)

(continued)

1989–1990

Numerous witnesses in Marina Del Rey, California, observe an object 100 feet in diameter moving swiftly back and forth underwater, just off the coast. In several cases, the large object ejects smaller USOs. In a few cases, lights emerge from the ocean and the object flies off into space.

While some UFO researchers shy away from accounts of UFO crashes as being too unbelievable and hard to prove, other researchers feel that these types of cases are among the most important of all UFO cases, and that they have the potential to provide definite proof that alien vehicles visit Earth. If these cases are valid, then sooner or later the truth will come out.

6

Conspiracies and Cover-ups

Frustrated by the lack of definitive proof that UFOs are alien spacecraft, many investigators claim that there is an official cover-up of the evidence. To support their assertions, investigators point out the many absurd explanations given by the Air Force to debunk UFO sightings. For example, the Air Force explained away the Hillsdale, Michigan, sightings as "swamp gas." Another reason investigators believe there is a cover-up is because many military insiders, such as those who have commented on the Roswell case, claim that the government is withholding crashed UFO hardware.

So, the question must be asked: What does the United States government know about UFOs? As it turns out, the United States government has taken the subject of UFOs very seriously. In fact, the Air Force, the **CIA**, and other governmental institutions have conducted large-scale official UFO studies.

PROJECT BLUE BOOK

Project Blue Book is probably the most famous government study of UFOs. It was started in 1952 by the United States Air Force, following a wave of sightings over the nation's capital. The study was headed in Dayton, Ohio, by Major Edward Ruppelt, the purpose being to determine if UFOs represented any threat to "national security."

For the next 17 years, the group of Air Force officers collected more than 12,618 reports of UFO sightings. The great majority of these sightings were believed to be the result of natural phenomena. Despite this, 701 of the cases remained unexplained and unidentified. The official conclusion of the study was that "No UFO reported, investigated, and evaluated by the Air Force has ever given any indication of threat to our National Security."

Researchers, however, have pointed out that UFO reports that affect national security actually bypassed Blue Book. According to official government documents, " . . . reports of unidentified flying objects that could affect national security are made in accordance with JANAP 146 or Air Force Manual 15-11, and are not a part of the Blue Book system." It turns out that JANAP 146 is a military regulation that forbids the public disclosure of UFO information. Imposed on both military and commercial pilots, disobeying this order can lead to a maximum of 10 years in jail and a fine of $10,000.

Today, investigators believe that Project Blue Book was a publicity stunt, and was used by the Air Force to wash their hands of the UFO problem. Even Ruppelt complained, saying, "Everything was being evaluated on the premise that UFOs couldn't exist." J. Allen Hynek was Project Blue Book's astronomical consultant. He wrote, "All my association with Blue Book showed clearly that the project rarely exhibited any interest in the UFO problem." Blue Book was shut down in 1969, and since then, the Air Force claims to have no interest in UFOs.[38]

THE CONDON COMMITTEE

Another well-known government study of UFOs was known as the **Condon Committee**, headed by Edward Condon and Robert Low. The study began after the famous Hillsdale, Michigan, sightings that the Air Force explained away as swamp gas. When the public refused to accept this explanation, the Air Force responded with the Condon

Committee. They gave the University of Colorado $313,000 dollars to conduct a two-year study.

Unfortunately, the study was doomed from the start. Edward Condon's ability to be objective was questioned when he announced, "My attitude right now is that there's nothing to it . . . but I'm not supposed to reach a conclusion for another year." On December 17, 1969, the study was closed down, with a negative conclusion on the existence of UFOs.

The methods and conclusions of the Condon Committee came under immediate attack. The American Institute of Aeronautics and Astronautics rejected the conclusions outright, saying, "We find it difficult to ignore the small residue of well-documented but unexplainable cases that form the hard core of the UFO controversy."

John Northrop of Northrop Aircraft said that the study was "one of the most deliberate cover-ups ever perpetrated on the public."

Figure 6.1 *Edward Condon (right), leader of the Condon Committee, which controversially denied the existence of UFOs.* (Hulton-Deutsch Collection/Corbis)

Several members of the committee actually resigned because of the controversy. Today, many investigators feel that the Condon Committee was—like Project Blue Book—more of a publicity stunt than an actual investigation.[39]

Presidential UFO Quotes

Although the United States government has officially denied the existence of UFOs, many highly placed officials have admitted that they actually believe in UFOs. This includes even presidents of the United States.

"I can assure you that flying saucers, given that they exist, are not constructed by any power on Earth."

—*President Harry S. Truman*

"I am convinced that UFOs exist because I've seen one . . . . It was the darndest thing I've ever seen. It was big; it was very bright; it changed colors; and it was about the size of the moon. We watched it for 10 minutes, but none of us could figure out what it was."

—*President Jimmy Carter*

"In the firm belief that the American public deserves a better explanation than that thus far given by the Air Force, I strongly recommend that there be a committee investigation of the UFO phenomena."

—*President Gerald Ford*

"If suddenly there was a threat to this world from some other species from another planet, we'd forget all the little local differences that we have between our two countries [U.S. and U.S.S.R.], and we would find out once and for all that we are all human beings on the Earth together."

—*President Ronald Reagan*

THE ROBERTSON PANEL

The Central Intelligence Agency (CIA) began its own official investigation into UFOs on January 12, 1953, with the creation of the **Robertson Panel**. It was composed of five major scientists, and was headed by Dr. Howard Percy Robertson.

Incredibly, the panel spent only five days on the study. They examined only 50 UFO cases–all taken from the files of Project Blue Book. Not surprisingly, the conclusions of the study were the same as Blue Book, saying that UFOs represented " . . . no direct physical threat to National Security." The ultimate result of the Robertson Panel was that the CIA ordered the Air Force to begin a "debunking" program to "strip the Unidentified Flying Objects of the special status they have been given and the aura of mystery they have unfortunately acquired."

While the CIA officially ended their UFO study with the Robertson Panel, documents released through the Freedom of Information Act tell a different story. Researchers Lawrence Fawcett and Barry Greenwood obtained several CIA documents dating through the 1970s proving that the CIA was still actively studying UFOs. Again, it seems, the public was being misled.[40]

THE FBI AND THE NSA

Many other governmental institutions have conducted official UFO studies. The Federal Bureau of Investigation (FBI) at first denied any involvement. However, in 1978 more than 1,700 pages of FBI UFO files were released, again indicating that the U.S. government is deeply interested in UFOs.

Even the *New York Times* couldn't deny the evidence, saying, "Though officials have long denied that they take 'flying saucers' seriously, declassified documents now reveal extensive government concern over the phenomenon."

The National Security Agency (**NSA**) has also denied having any interest in UFOs, and yet again, government documents tell a different story. Proof of the UFO cover-up came in 1980, when the private UFO group, Citizens Against UFO Secrecy (**CAUS**) used the Freedom of Information Act to force the NSA to release any UFO documents it was holding. The United States District Court heard the case of CAUS vs. NSA. The court reviewed a 21-page Top Secret report about the alleged documents because the NSA felt that the documents themselves were too sensitive to release even to the courts.

Citizens Against UFO Secrecy discovered that the NSA had 239 UFO documents. However, the court ruled in favor of the NSA. They refused to release the documents saying that such an action "could seriously jeopardize the work of the agency and the security of the United States." The court concluded that, "Public interest in disclosure is far out-weighed by the sensitive nature of the materials and the obvious effect on national security their release would entail."[41]

UFOS AND THE UNITED STATES CONGRESS

On July 28, 1968, the first Congressional hearings were held on the subject of UFOs. Distinguished scientists from across the country were asked to testify before the House Committee on Science and Astronautics. Nearly all the scientists recommended further investigation into the phenomenon.

Panel member Dr. J. Allen Hynek said, "As far as UFOs are concerned, I believe we should investigate them for the simple reason that we want to know what lies behind this utterly baffling phenomenon."

Famous astronomer Carl Sagan agreed, and said, "If we are being visited by representatives of extraterrestrial life, just to stick our heads in the sand would be a very bad policy, I think."

Dr. Robert Hall testified, "There is strong evidence that there is some physical phenomena underlying a portion of the reports."[42]

While the overall conclusion of the Congressional hearings was positive, it had little effect. Today, the government officially does not investigate UFO reports. However, many civilian UFO researchers

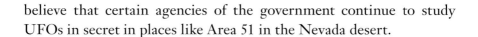

believe that certain agencies of the government continue to study UFOs in secret in places like Area 51 in the Nevada desert.

AREA 51 AND MJ-12

In 1989, a physicist by the name of Bob Lazar went public with an incredible story. He claimed to have worked on secret government projects involving crashed UFOs. He said that the area known as Groom Lake, or Area 51, located in the Nevada desert above Las Vegas, was actually a secret government base used to "reverse-engineer" alien spacecraft. He said that he and hundreds of other scientists were trying to figure out how the UFOs worked and were actually flying them, too. He said that there were several different types of E.T. craft hidden at Area 51, and that they were so advanced that even the leading scientists had trouble figuring them out. Lazar was unable to prove his story, but before long, other scientists, such as Bill Uhouse, Doug Schroeder, and others, also came forward, saying that UFOs were being held and studied at the base. The rumors spread and, before long, crowds of UFO hunters converged on the outskirts of the base, observing and filming apparent UFOs coming in and out of the base. The objects were usually seen late at night. They looked like fiery globes of light, which would hover silently and sometimes dart at right angles or accelerate at high speeds.

Officially, Area 51 doesn't even exist. However, the entire area is restricted to public entry, and as signs all around the base read: "No Trespassing: Use of Deadly Force is Authorized."

On April 19, 1996, the governor of Nevada officially named Highway 375—which runs along the southern border of the 6,200 square mile base—the "Extraterrestrial Highway." Even today, enthusiasts still gather at the famous "Little Ale'Inn" restaurant in nearby Rachel, Nevada, hoping to see a human-piloted UFO.

Another area often mentioned with the UFO cover-up is known as Hangar 18, located at Wright-Patterson Air Force base in Dayton,

The Mysterious Men in Black

A very mysterious aspect of the UFO phenomenon is known as the **Men in Black**, or MIBs. There are apparently two types of MIBs. The first type are secret government agents, such as those portrayed in the popular movie *Men in Black*, starring Will Smith and Tommy Lee Jones.

The second type of MIBs, however, are not government agents at all; they are apparently extraterrestrials. They often arrive in shiny black Cadillacs. They don't walk normally, but kind of shuffle along. They dress in identical black suits and have very pale skin and weird, dark eyes. They talk in a strange accent that witnesses sometimes describe as robotic. Strangest of all, they may literally appear or disappear right before the witnesses' eyes.

Both types of Men in Black have appeared on the scene following dramatic UFO encounters that involve some type of physical evidence. The MIB usually confront the UFO witness, demand the evidence, and then threaten the witness not to talk about the UFO encounter.

The first recorded case can be traced back to 1953 when UFO investigator Albert K. Bender was visited by the MIB and threatened to stop his research. Bender was so scared that he retired from UFO investigations. Since then there have been dozens of similar cases. Some UFO witnesses and researchers report weird phone problems or harassment by unmarked black helicopters. While many people have been threatened, nobody has apparently been hurt. Today, the origins of the MIB phenomenon remain unknown. Those who see a UFO and take a

Ohio. Researcher Leonard Stringfield claims to have spoken with dozens of firsthand witnesses who say that Hangar 18 is where much of the crashed UFO hardware is being held and studied. One lady told Stringfield that it was her job to label and categorize each item

Figure 6.2 *The Men in Black, or MIB, are nefarious characters who sometimes appear after a UFO encounter, threatening the witnesses not to talk about what they saw. Most eyewitnesses believe the MIB are some type of E.T.* (Kesara Art)

photograph should be prepared for a possible visit from the mysterious Men in Black.

as it came in. She was made to sign a top-secret agreement to keep silent, and only revealed her story on her deathbed. Today, many other researchers have also uncovered similar stories about Hangar 18. Stringfield published his findings in a series of privately published

Figure 6.3 *This photo was taken in Rachel, Nevada, near the secret U.S. military installation known as Area 51.* (Mark Peterson/Corbis)

"Status Reports." Unfortunately, most of the witnesses to Hangar 18 have insisted upon remaining anonymous, making it difficult to prove their stories. However, more indications of the UFO cover-up come from other areas.

Further evidence that the government is allegedly studying UFOs in secret comes from a set of leaked government documents called the "MJ-12 papers." In the late 1980s, these documents were sent anonymously to several UFO researchers. The documents said that the Roswell UFO crash did, in fact, occur, and that after the incident, President Harry S. Truman organized a panel of 12 leading scientists and military officials to handle the UFO situation. It was the job of the people working on MJ-12 to obtain all crashed UFOs and alien bodies, to study the alien technology, and to keep everything top secret. Researcher Stanton Friedman and others have analyzed the documents in detail, checking for contradictions in style, dates, terms, signatures, anything that would prove or disprove their authenticity. All their research pointed toward the documents being genuine. Says Friedman, "Surprisingly, nothing that we had found, or that others had alleged, indicated that the documents were anything other than legitimate."[43]

7

UFO Hoaxes

On July 2, 1950, a young couple was fishing at Steep Rock Lake in Ontario, Canada, when they noticed a "large shiny object" floating on the far shoreline. Several 4-foot-tall figures stood on top of the craft. One of the figures pulled out a strange green hose and began to suck water out of the lake and into the craft. After several minutes, the figures returned into the craft, and the object took off. An amazing case, by any standards. In fact, the account was a sensation, and later made it into several popular UFO books. The only problem is, it never happened. It turns out that the entire story was made up as a joke. Like many hoaxes, events escalated and quickly got out of control before the hoax could be revealed.[44]

As the "Steep Rock Hoax" case shows, UFO investigation can be a tricky business. Anybody can claim to have encountered a UFO. But how do investigators know who is telling the truth? Is it possible that some UFO reports are the results of hoaxes?

Of course, some UFO reports are generated by pranksters. What many people don't realize is that UFO hoaxes can be very damaging to the field of UFO research for several reasons. First, they waste the valuable time of UFO researchers as they are forced to track down the truth. Second, they pollute the field with false information and divert attention away from genuine cases. Finally, they result in the public perception that most UFO cases are caused by hoaxes, when in fact UFO hoaxes are relatively rare.

Investigator Antonio Huneeus conducted a study of dozens of UFO hoaxes. Writes Huneeus, "The few official studies undertaken on the UFO phenomenon have shown hoaxes not to be statistically significant. Out of the total of 13,134 UFO reports collected by the Air Force's Project Blue Book and its predecessors between 1947 and 1969, only 116 cases, or 0.9 percent, were labeled hoaxes."

Even though hoaxes are rare, ufologists have learned the hard way to be very careful when evaluating UFO reports. Thankfully, most hoaxes can be uncovered by an in-depth investigation. UFO cases that may seem solid at first suddenly fall apart under close examination. Witnesses may change their story. Physical evidence turns out to be false. Even UFO photographs can be faked.

Fortunately, most hoaxes are revealed before they can do much damage. However, every now and then, a spectacular UFO case makes it into the record, and then later turns out to be a hoax. For this reason, investigators cannot be too careful. One typical example is known as the "Alien Autopsy."

THE ALIEN AUTOPSY

In 1996, filmmaker Ray Santilli electrified the world with the release of footage showing the autopsy of an alleged extraterrestrial being. The footage was said to have been purchased from an anonymous cameraman who claimed the film showed one of the aliens from the Roswell UFO crash. The film was sold to the Fox Network and aired several times in a television special.

The film itself was shocking. It showed a human-looking figure lying dead on a table. While the figure did have two arms, two legs, and a head, any similarity to a human being ended there. The figure had six fingers on each hand, large dark eyes, white skin, and an abnormally large, bald head. The film showed two doctors cutting into the body and removing several organs.

Figure 7.1 *This "UFO sighting" was faked using a model UFO.* (Fortean Picture Library)

Figure 7.2 *Paul Villa claimed to have photographed UFOs on several occasions, this one near Albuquerque, New Mexico on June 16, 1963. The photograph was later shown to be fake.* (Fortean Picture Library)

Screen Memories: Cases of Alien Hoaxing

While humans sometimes put on UFO hoaxes, what many people don't know is that aliens also sometimes try to hoax humans! These cases are known as **screen memories**. Many UFO investigators believe that aliens will sometimes hypnotize witnesses during an encounter and make them think that they are seeing something other than aliens. The reason for this is uncertain, but most investigators think that it is done by the E.T.s in an attempt to hide themselves from humans, or perhaps to reduce the level of fear that some witnesses experience during close encounters. Some of the most common disguises used by the E.T.s include owls, deer, wolves, spiders, clowns—even stuffed animals.

One example of aliens disguising themselves happened to UFO abductee Whitley Strieber. During one of his many encounters, he was stunned to see what he thought was an impossibly large owl staring in his bedroom window. Later, under hypnosis, he was able to see through the disguise and observe the aliens in their true form: as short gray beings with large hairless heads and huge dark eyes.

The lesson is clear: With aliens and UFOs, things are not always what they appear to be.

Almost immediately, skeptics attacked the film. Even UFO researchers became divided about its authenticity. Believers pointed out that the film was dated to 1947, and there were no inconsistencies to show that this wasn't the truth. However, skeptics claimed that the film was amateurish and could be easily faked with special effects. The controversy raged for years, with both sides presenting convincing arguments for their case. Then in 2006, Ray Santilli said that he believed the film was a fake. And there the case ends. However, even now, some investigators still believe in the case, pointing out that there is still no proof of a hoax. Thus the controversy continues.[45]

THE GREATEST UFO HOAX IN HISTORY

The dangers of hoaxing a UFO encounter are illustrated perfectly by what happened in 1938, in Grovers Mill, New Jersey. On the evening of October 31, 1938, a young radio director named Orson Welles presented the fictional sci-fi story *War of the Worlds* (about aliens landing on Earth) as if it were an actual news broadcast. Welles gave a documentary-style report, saying that aliens had landed at the small town of Grovers Mills, and that the police, the U.S. Army, and other officials had arrived and were being overtaken by the more powerful E.T.s. Despite the fact that the broadcast was interrupted by frequent station breaks declaring that the invasion was only a "dramatization," many people believed the reports to be true. Across New Jersey and parts of New York, Pennsylvania, Delaware, and other nearby states, panic allegedly ensued as citizens prepared for an alien invasion. Some reacted by fleeing their homes and heading for the hills, while others armed themselves with weapons and supplies and prepared to fight the encroaching E.T.s. The radio station and local police were swamped with angry and frightened callers, demanding more information.

The dramatic response of the citizens of New Jersey and New York stunned the world, and Orson Welles became famous overnight for having pulled off a UFO hoax that fooled an estimated one million people. The Federal Communications Commission forced Welles to make a public apology, which he did. However, the broadcast made his career, and Welles went on to became one of the leading filmmakers of all time. Welles, however, was the exception. Most people who hoax a UFO event soon learn to regret their mistake.

Figure 7.3 *H.G. Wells (left), author of* War of the Worlds, *photographed with Orson Welles (right), perpetrator of the famous UFO radio hoax that depicted Wells's sci-fi story as if it were really happening.* (Bettmann/Corbis)

OTHER UFO HOAXES

Unfortunately, the UFO field has been plagued by dozens of other hoaxes. On January 23, 1967, a young boy from Florham Park, New

Jersey, decided to play a joke on his friends. He built a model of a flying saucer, dangled it outside his bedroom window, and took a photograph. The photo turned out to be very convincing. At first it seemed like a harmless prank. But when several adults believed in the case, and then the next day the photograph appeared in the newspapers, things got out of hand. The police and other investigators became involved, and the witness was forced to reveal that he had hoaxed the entire incident. What started as a joke turned out to be a big embarrassment.

Many UFO hoaxes involve photographs, usually of a UFO or an alien body. The reason for this is because most UFO cases involve no physical evidence. Hoaxsters apparently believe that a photograph will convince people that their case is genuine. UFO photographs may be easy to fake, but they are also easy to detect.

One of the most famous examples of this kind occurred on May 8, 1988, when Puerto Rican hotdog vendor Amaury Rivera claimed to have been abducted by E.T.s. In support of his story, he produced several clear photographs of a UFO being chased by a Navy F-14 Tomcat jet fighter. The case electrified the UFO community, and the story and photos were widely published.

A few months later, however, the truth was revealed. Wilson Sosa, the lead investigator who had originally supported the case, now declared that it was a hoax. It turned out that inconsistencies in the photographs (including shadows and other technical details) revealed that Amaury Rivera, who had sold his photos for thousands of dollars to various media outlets, had actually faked the entire incident using models. Professional photographer Manuel Fernandez also analyzed the photos and agreed that they were hoaxed. Writes Fernandez, "The photos are false and two small models were utilized to make them."

Another striking UFO photograph that turned out to be a fake was first revealed by Russian cosmonaut Marina Popovich at a 1980 UFO conference in Munich, Germany. In this case, the photograph showed the body of an alleged gray-type E.T., supposedly one of the aliens recovered from Roswell. The E.T. in the photo had huge eyes, a large hairless head, a small nose and mouth, gray skin, and was wearing a silver jumpsuit. However, investigators raised questions from the beginning when they noticed that the jumpsuit had a conventional-looking zipper on the front. It was later discovered that the photograph was taken at a Montreal exhibit in the late 1970s, and the "alien" was actually just a plastic dummy.

At least a half-dozen other hoaxed, plastic-dummy alien photographs have come and gone through the years, again making it very difficult for the investigator to separate the truth from the fiction.[46]

Yet another hoax occurred in the summer of 1992, when dozens of people in Sydney, Australia, called the police to report strange orange balls of light hovering in formations. UFO investigators collected the reports and spread the word about the new UFO wave. Soon, however, it was learned that the UFOs were actually garbage bags that had been sent aloft by teenagers using candles to fill the bags with hot air. Unfortunately, the faked UFOs were so convincing that several UFO investigators were fooled, and the accounts made it into the newspapers before finally being revealed as a hoax.[47]

Many other hoax cases are on record, including cases of faked UFO abductions and even UFO crashes. No UFO story should be accepted without first checking the facts and conducting a thorough investigation.

Conclusions

We have now examined the UFO phenomenon from the beginning of recorded history to the present day. We have traveled through time and across the world and seen how UFOs have been encountered for thousands of years. We have examined many of the world's most famous and best authenticated sightings. We have studied landing trace cases, photographic evidence, and medical evidence. We have gone inside the UFOs and learned about the aliens said to pilot these strange devices. We have even heard reports of UFO crash/retrievals and secret government UFO studies.

After all of this, what have we learned? Can we draw any solid conclusions about the UFO phenomenon?

One conclusion that can be drawn is that UFOs—whatever they are—are part of a real phenomenon. People are definitely seeing something. The physical evidence includes photographs, moving films, radar-returns, **landing traces**, metal fragments, medical effects, electromagnetic effects, and multiple eyewitness testimonies supported by lie-detector tests and more.

Another conclusion that can be drawn is that UFOs appear to represent a superior technology. In case after case, the UFOs fly circles around the most advanced man-made aircraft. They can hover in space, move in and out of water, turn at right angles, and travel at thousands of miles per hour. They can abduct people out of their cars and homes, and we seem to be powerless to stop them.

Unfortunately, none of this actually explains exactly what UFOs are. The most popular theory is that UFOs are extraterrestrial spacecraft. Certainly this theory seems to account for most of the evidence.

However, it is not the only theory. As we have seen, some other theories include time travelers from the future, interdimensional beings, or even creatures from the inner Earth. With so many different types of aliens, even UFO researchers remain undecided about UFO origins. And then there are the reports of angels, fairies, elves, and other supernatural creatures. Are these aliens, or are they something else entirely? When it comes to UFOs, only one thing is certain: The phenomenon is not going away. UFOs have been around for centuries and are still being encountered today. A recent case occurred on March 5, 2004, when the Mexican Air Force filmed multiple UFOs over Mexico, using infrared film. Although the objects were invisible to the naked eye, they also registered on radar. The sighting was front-page news. Nobody was able to explain the incident. Another recent case occurred on November 7, 2006, when pilots and air-traffic controllers sighted a gray, metallic, saucer-shaped object over O'Hare Airport in Chicago. The object hovered briefly over the airport before zooming upward into the sky, punching a hole in the clouds. Again, the incident made front-page news, and again nobody was able to explain the incident. Until UFOs make open contact with humanity, we will be left with more questions than answers. Until that day, UFOs will remain a mystery.

Timeline

Prehistory   Cave art and sculptures depict UFOs and E.T.-type figures; myths in different cultures tell of wise beings who came from the sky

BC–1890s   Early manuscripts, records, and paintings show evidence of unknown aerial objects across the world

1896   Strange zeppelin-like airships are sighted across the United States

June 30, 1909   Huge explosion occurs over Tunguska, Russia: cause unknown

February 25, 1942   Los Angeles Air Raid; U.S. military shoots at UFO as it hovers over Culver City, California

1943–1944   Small balls of light called foo fighters are observed by fighter pilots of World War II

1946–1947   Sweden and nearby countries are plagued by wave of "ghost rockets"

June 24, 1947   Pilot Kenneth Arnold sights UFOs over Mount Rainier, Washington, starting the Modern Age of UFOs

July 4, 1947   UFO allegedly crashes outside of Roswell, New Mexico; evidence is reportedly covered up by the U.S. military

July 7, 1947   Edwards Air Force Base in southern California experiences a wave of sightings directly over the base

January 8, 1948   Captain Mantell fatally crashes his plane while in pursuit of a UFO over Louisville, Kentucky

July 25, 1948   Pilots Charles and Whitted nearly collide with a UFO while flying from Texas to Georgia

October 1, 1948 Pilot Gorman chases a UFO over Fargo, North Dakota

May 11, 1950 Paul Trent photographs UFO over McMinnville, Oregon

July 2, 1950 UFO hoax is perpetrated at Steeprock Lake in Ontario, Canada

August 15, 1950 Nick Mariana films several bright objects near Great Falls, Montana; Analysis of the footage shows that they are unexplained

August 25, 1951 A UFO wave sweeps over the town of Lubbock, Texas

1952 United States Air Force opens Project Blue Book, to collect and study UFO reports

July 15, 1952 Multiple UFOs are sighted over Washington DC

August 23, 1952 Scoutmaster Sonny Desvergers is burned by beam of light from a UFO in Florida Everglades

September 12, 1952 UFO lands in Flatwoods, Virginia; robotic figure is seen

November 20, 1952 George Adamski claims to make contact with an extraterrestrial in Desert Center, California

February–June, 1952 UFO lands at Brush Creek, California; small dwarf-like E.T. observed

January 1953 The CIA funds "The Robertson Panel" UFO study, which recommends debunking the subject of UFOs

March 22, 1953 Sara Shaw and Jan Whitley are abducted by gray-type E.T.s into a UFO in Tujunga, California, but the case remains unknown for twenty years

August–October 1954 France experiences an intense UFO wave

September 10, 1954 UFO lands in Quarouble, France, leaving physical traces

August 22, 1955 The Sutton family of Hopkinsville, Kentucky shoots at dwarf-like E.T.

October 7, 1957 First reported UFO abduction: farmer Antonio Villas Boas is abducted into a UFO outside of Saõ Paolo, Brazil (account not released publicly)

November 5, 1957 A UFO with humanoid occupants is observed landed on the beach at Playa Del Rey

January 6 1958 Brazilian Navy photographs UFO over Trinidade Island

June 26–27, 1959 Dozens of witnesses observe a UFO with occupants hover over a mission in Papua, New Guinea

August 13–19, 1960 Northern California experiences a week-long intense UFO wave; witnesses include dozens of police officers

April 18, 1961 UFO lands at Eagle River, Wisconsin; human-looking E.T.s give farmer "alien pancakes"

September 19, 1961 Betty and Barney Hill are abducted into a UFO in New Hampshire, and become the first people to publicly report a UFO abduction

April 24, 1964 UFO lands in farmer's field in Tioga, New York; human-like E.T.s ask for fertilizer

April 24, 1964 Police Officer Lonnie Zamora observes a landed UFO and occupants in Socorro, New Mexico; UFO leaves landing traces

September 4, 1964 UFO lands in Cisco Grove, California; robotic-like E.T. traps hunter in tree

January 30, 1965 Radio technician Sid Padrick of Watsonville California is invited aboard a UFO by friendly, human-looking E.T.s

June 4, 1965 Astronaut McDivitt films UFO outside Gemini IV capsule

August 3, 1965 Highway inspector Rex Heflin photographs a UFO over Santa Ana, California

December 9, 1965 A UFO allegedly crashes outside of Kecksburg, Pennsylvania; military forces reportedly recover the object

1965–1966 The town of Exeter, New Hampshire experiences an intense UFO wave involving citizens, police officers, and UFO investigators

March 18–22, 1966 More than 100 people observe UFOs in Hillsdale and Dexter, Michigan

April 17, 1966 Police deputies Spaur and Neff chase a UFO across Ohio and Pennsylvania

1966-1967 UFO wave sweeps across the rural communities in the Uintah Basin in central Utah. At the same time, more than 100 residents in the small town of Point Pleasant, West Virginia report encounters with UFOs and a strange bat-like creature called "the Mothman"

1967 The United States Air Force funds the Condon Committee to conduct an official UFO study; study is shut down after two years

January 25, 1967 Housewife Betty Andreasson is abducted by gray-type E.T.s into a UFO from her home in Ashburnham, Massachusetts

May 20, 1967 Stephen Michalek is burned by a landed UFO in Falcon Lake, Canada

October 4, 1967 Multiple witnesses observe a UFO crash into Shag Harbor, Canada; incident is confirmed by official documents

September 9, 1967 First animal mutilation reported in San Luis Valley, Colorado; case involves the unexplained death of a horse

December 3, 1967 Police Officer Herbert Schirmer is abducted into a UFO by human-looking E.T.s in Ashland, Nebraska

July 28, 1968 Official Congressional Hearings are held on the subject of UFOs

1969 United States Air Force closes down Project Blue Book

October 1969 Georgia Governor Jimmy Carter sees a UFO over Georgia while campaigning to become president of the United States

November 2, 1971 UFO lands in Delphos, Kansas; UFO leaves landing traces

October 11, 1973   Fishermen Parker and Hickson are abducted by robotic-like creatures into a UFO in Pascagoula, Mississippi

October 18, 1973   Captain Coyne encounters UFO over Columbus, Ohio

October 25, 1974   Hunter Carl Higdon is abducted by human-looking E.T.s into a UFO in Rawlins, Wyoming

August 13, 1975   Sergeant Charles Moody is abducted into a UFO by almost-human-looking E.T.s outside of Alamogordo, New Mexico

November 5, 1975   Woodcutter Travis Walton is abducted into a UFO and is missing for five days

January 20, 1976   Three ladies are abducted by short humanoids into a UFO outside of Liberty, Kentucky

August 24, 1976   Four campers are abducted into a UFO while canoeing outside of Allagash, Maine

October 21, 1978   Pilot Frederick Valentich disappears after a close encounter with a UFO off the coast of Melbourne, Australia

December 26–29, 1980   UFO lands next to military base in Rendlesham, England; official documents and landing traces confirm the event

December 29, 1980   Three witnesses receive radiation-like burns from a UFO over Huffman, Texas; unmarked black helicopters observed

1982–1984   The Hudson Valley area of upstate New York experiences a UFO wave involving large triangular-shaped craft

December 11, 1984   MJ-12 papers are leaked to researchers, revealing the alleged existence of a secret governmental UFO study group

October 4 & December 25, 1985   Author Whitley Strieber is abducted by gray-type E.T.s from his cabin in upstate New York

November 17, 1986   The crew of a Japanese commercial airliner encounters multiple UFOs while over Alaska; objects are observed on radar

1987   Researcher Budd Hopkins releases his landmark book, *Intruders*, which claims that E.T.s are interested in human genetics

1987–1988   A UFO wave sweeps across the small town of Wytheville, Virginia

1987–1992   Gulf Breeze, Florida experiences five-year-long UFO wave; contractor Ed Walters photographs the UFOs

January 20, 1988   The Knowles family of four is lifted up in their car by a UFO while driving through Nullabor, Australia

1989   Physicist Bob Lazar and others reveal the existence of Area 51 outside of Las Vegas, the alleged location of recovered flying saucers

September 27, 1989   Dozens of children observe a landed UFO with occupants in a field in Voronezh, Russia

November 30, 1989   Linda Napolitano is abducted from her apartment in Brooklyn, New York; event is observed by outside witnesses

1989–1992   Belgium experiences an intense wave of UFO activity involving a large, triangular-shaped object

July 11, 1991   UFO is sighted by thousands of residents over Mexico City, Mexico; dozens of people videotape the object

June 13–17, 1992   The Massachusetts Institute of Technology (MIT) holds a scientific conference to study the subject of UFO abductions

1992–1994   The town of Topanga Canyon, California experiences a two-year-long wave of activity involving the full range of encounters from sightings to UFO abductions

August 8, 1993   Kelly Cahill and several others are abducted into a UFO by tall humanoid E.T.s in Victoria, Australia

1994   Pulitzer Prize-winning author and Harvard Professor John Mack, MD releases his groundbreaking book, *Abduction*

August 8, 1995   Alien autopsy footage is aired publicly; most investigators believe it was a hoax

August 19, 1995   Dr. Roger Leir performs first of several "alien implant" removal surgeries in Ventura, California

January 20, 1996   UFO with strange occupants is seen outside of Varginha, Brazil; Brazilian military allegedly captures two of the E.T.s

March 13, 1997   Huge V-shaped craft sighted by thousands of people over Phoenix, Arizona; object is filmed and photographed

January 5, 2000   A large box-like UFO is seen by multiple police officers moving over central Illinois

March 5, 2004   Mexican Air Force uses radar and infrared photography to detect several unidentified flying objects

Glossary

ABDUCTEES   People who claim to have been taken by extraterrestrials aboard a UFO; also known as contactees

ALIEN IMPLANT   A device allegedly placed by extraterrestrials inside the human body for as of yet unknown reasons

AREA 51   An area in the Nevada desert north of Las Vegas where the United States government is allegedly studying extraterrestrial craft

CAUS   Citizens Against UFO Secrecy

CIA   Central Intelligence Agency

CONDON COMMITTEE   An official UFO study conducted by the United States Air Force (1966–1969)

ELECTROMAGNETIC EFFECTS   UFO-caused disturbances to electrically-powered devices, including: power-failures, car engine stalling, radio and/or television static, car headlights dimming, watches stopping, cameras jamming, batteries losing power, and other malfunctions which occur to machines in the presence of a UFO

FBI   Federal Bureau of Investigation

FLYING SAUCER   See UFO

"FOO FIGHTERS"   Small balls of light seen following the planes of World War II fighter pilots

FREEDOM OF INFORMATION ACT   Used by UFO researchers to obtain formerly classified United States Government UFO documents

GRAYS   Humanoid alien described as three to five feet in height and having a large, hairless head, gray skin, and dark, almond-shaped eyes

HYPNOSIS   A psychological technique used by psychologists to retrieve memories that have been buried in the subconscious

LANDING TRACES   Marks, burns, or impressions on the ground and surrounding vegetation caused by the landing of UFO

MEN IN BLACK   Figures described as human-looking except wearing dark suits, dark sunglasses, with very pale skin, weird eyes, and strange accents; in most cases, they show up after a UFO encounter, demanding to be given any physical evidence and threatening witnesses not to speak; UFO investigators remain unsure whether they are extraterrestrials or human, or if there are two types

MISSING TIME   A period of amnesia experienced by a witness during a close-up UFO sighting; believed by UFO investigators to be an indication of an unremembered onboard experience

MOGUL BALLOON   A formerly classified weather and observation balloon used by the United States Air Force

MUFON   The Mutual UFO Network, a civilian UFO study group (see reference section)

NORDICS   A human-looking alien, often blond-haired

NSA   National Security Agency

PLEIADIAN   A human-looking alien, allegedly originating from the Pleiades

PRAYING MANTIS   Insectoid alien with the appearance of a giant grasshopper or praying mantis, usually described as being between six to eight feet tall, with large dark eyes and claw-like appendages

PROJECT BLUE BOOK   An official study of the UFO phenomenon conducted by the United States Air Force (1952–1969)

REPTILION   A lizard-type E.T. usually described as being eight to ten feet in height, a lizard-like face, very muscular, with scales covering the entire body; also known as reptoid

ROBERTSON PANEL   Official study of the UFO phenomenon conducted by the United States Central Intelligence Agency in January 1953

ROBOTS   A UFO occupant that appears to be an artificially constructed machine as opposed to a living being

SCREEN MEMORIES   False memories (often of animals such as deer, owl, wolves) that have been allegedly placed into the mind of a UFO witness by extraterrestrials to cover-up the memory of an actual UFO event

TELEPATHY   Direct communication from mind to mind, often experienced by people who have face-to-face contact with extraterrestrials

UFO   Unidentified flying object(s) often used to denote extraterrestrial spacecraft; also known as flying saucer

USAF   United States Air Force

ZETA-RETICULI   Star system (identified through the Betty and Barney Hill case) believed to be the home location of at least one species of gray-type extraterrestrial

Endnotes

1. Time-Life Editors, *The UFO Phenomenon* (Alexandria, Va.: Time-Life Books, Inc, 1987), 13; Jacques Vallee, *Anatomy of a Phenomenon: UFOs in Space* (New York: Ballantine Books, 1965), 1–11.

2. Richard Thompson, *Alien Identities* (San Diego, Calif.: Govardhan Hill Publishing, 1993), 257; Brinsley Le Poer Trench, *The Flying Saucer Story* (New York: Ace Books, Inc., 1966), 81–82; Jacques Vallee, *The Invisible College* (New York: E. P. Dutton, 1975), 128–131.

3. Harold T. Wilkins, *Flying Saucers on the Attack* (New York: Ace Books, Inc., 1954), 165–185.

4. Harold E. Burt, *Flying Saucers 101: Everything You Ever Wanted to Know About Unidentified Flying Objects* (Sunland, Calif.: UFO Magazine, Inc., 2000), 27; Wilkins, *Flying Saucers on the Attack*, 187–195; Carl Jung, *Flying Saucers: A Modern Myth of Things Seen in the Sky* (Princeton, N.J.: Princeton/Bollingen Paperbacks, 1978), 95.

5. Ralph and Judy Blum, *Beyond Earth: Man's Contact with UFOs* (New York: Bantam Books, 1974), 49; Jacques Vallee, *Passport to Magonia: On UFOs, Folklore and Parallel Worlds*, 180; Wilkins, *Flying Saucers on the Attack*, 203.

6. Paris Flammonde, *UFO Exist* (New York: Ballantine Books, 1976), 134–136.; Timothy Good, *Above Top Secret: The Worldwide UFO Cover-up* (New York: William Morrow & Company, Inc., 1988), 18–19.

7. Good, *Above Top Secret: The World Wide Cover-up*, 19–23; Time-Life Editors, *The UFO Phenomenon*, 26.

8. Flammonde, *UFO Exist*, 172–173.

9. Good, *Above Top Secret: The Worldwide UFO Cover*-up, 262–263.

10. Flammonde, *UFO* Exist, 258–262.

11. Ibid., 313–316.

12. Captain Kevin D. Randle, USAFR, *Invasion Washington: UFOs Over the Capitol* (New York: HarperCollins Publishers, 2001), 32–42.

13. Flammonde, *UFO Exist*, 357–362.

14. Time-Life Editors, *The UFO Phenomenon*, 111–115.

15. Michael David Hall, *A Century of Sightings* (Lakeville, Minn.: Galde Press, 1999), 310–311.

16. Bill Chalker, *The Oz Files: The Australian UFO Story* (Potts Point, Australia: Duffy & Snellgrove, 1996), 183–189.

17. Lynn Kitei, *The Phoenix Lights* (Charlottesville, Va.: Hampton Roads, 2004), 12–24.

18. The Learning Channel (TLC), *UFOs Over Illinois: Anatomy of a Sighting*, 2006.

19. Frank Feschino Jr., *The Braxton County Monster: The Cover-up of the Flatwoods Monster Revealed* (Charleston, W.V.: Quarrier Press, 2004), 1–43.

20. Gray Barker, *They Knew Too Much About Flying Saucers* (New York: University Books, 1956), 36–58.

21. Aime Michel, *Flying Saucers and the Straight Line Mystery* (New York: Criterion Books, 1958), 44–47.

22. Coral and Jim Lorenzen, *Encounters With UFO Occupants* (New York: Berkley Publishing Corp., 1976), 174–175.

23. Ibid., 8–11; Good, *Above Top Secret: The Worldwide UFO Cover-up*, 343–345.

24. Good, *Above Top Secret: The Worldwide UFO Cover-up*, 195–204.

25. Dwight Connelly, *The World's Best UFO Cases* Martinsville, Ill.: Bookseller, Inc., 2004), 122–132.

26. Philip Mantle and Paul Stonehill, *Mysterious Sky: Soviet UFO Phenomenon* (Baltimore, Md.: www.publishamerica.com, 2006), 107–116.

27. Ann Druffel and D. Scott Rogo, *The Tujunga Canyon Contacts: Updated Edition* (New York: Signet Books, 1988), 3–64.

28. Lorenzen, *Encounters With UFO Occupants*, 61–87.

29. John G. Fuller, *The Interrupted Journey* (New York: Berkley Medallion Books, 1976), 61–87.

30. Charles Hickson and William Mendez, *UFO Contact at Pascagoula* (Tuczon, Ariz.: Wendelle C. Stevens, 1983), 7–166.

31. Coral and Jim Lorenzen, *Abducted: Confrontations with Beings From Outer Space* (New York: Berkley Medallion Books, 1977), 38–51.

32. Travis Walton, *The Walton Experience* (New York: Berkley Publishing Publishing Corp., 1978), 23–126.

33. Otto Billig, *Flying Saucers – Magic in the Skies* (Cambridge, Mass.: Shenkman Publishing Company, Inc., 1982), 15–30; Lorenzen, *Abducted!: Confrontations with Beings From Outer Space*, 285–330.

34. Whitley Strieber, *Communion: A True Story* (New York: William Morrow & Company, Inc., 1987), 1–178.

35. Charles Berlitz and William L. Moore, *The Roswell Incident* (New York: Berkley Books, 1988); Captain Kevin D. Randle, USAFR and Donald Schmitt, *The Truth About the UFO Crash at Roswell* (New York: M. Evans & Company, 1994), 3–113.

36. Ryan S. Wood, *Majic Eyes Only: Earth's Encounters with Extraterrestrial Technology* (Broomfield, Colo.: Wood Enterprises, 2005), 152–160.

37. Don Ledger and Chris Styles, *Dark Object: The World's Only Government-Documented UFO Crash* (New York: Dell Publishing, 2001), 1–168.

38. Good, *Above Top Secret: The Worldwide UFO Cover-up*, 264, 443; J. Allen Hynek, *The UFO Experience: A Scientific Inquiry* (New York:

Ballantine Books, 1987), 201; Brad Steiger, *Project Blue Book: The Top Secret UFO Findings Revealed* (New York: Ballantine Books, 1976), 214.

39. Flammonde, *UFO Exist*, 16, 411; Raymond E. Fowler, *UFOs: Interplanetary Visitors* (Englewood Cliffs, N.J.: Prentice-Hall, Inc., 1974), 157–159.

40. Lawrence Fawcett and Barry J. Greenwood, *Clear Intent: The Government Cover-up of the UFO Experience* (Englewood Cliffs, N.J.: Prentice-Hall, Inc., 1984), 126–149; Flammonde, *UFO Exist*, 42.

41. Fawcett and Greenwood, *Clear Intent: The Government Cover-up of the UFO Experience*, 124–149; Good, *Above Top Secret: The Worldwide UFO Cover-up*, 147.

42. John G. Fuller, *Aliens in the Skies: The New Battle of the Scientists*

(New York: Berkley Medallion Books, 1969), 56, 92–124.

43. Michael Hesemann and Philip Mantle, *Beyond Roswell: The Alien Autopsy Film, Area 51 & the U.S. Government Coverup of UFOs* (New York: Marlowe & Company, 1997), 152–163.

44. John Robert Colombo, *UFOs Over Canada* (Ontario, Canada: Hounslow Press, 1991), 32–41.

45. Michael Hesemann and Philip Mantle, *Beyond Roswell: The Alien Autopsy Film, Area 51 & the U.S. Government Cover-up of UFOs*, 269–286.

46. Antonio Huneeus, "UFO Hoaxes," *Fate* 47, no. 534 (September 1994): 36–41.

47. Chalker, *The Oz Files: The Australian UFO Story*, 86–94.

Further Resources

BOOKS

Dolan, Richard M. *UFOs and the National Security State: Chronology of a Cover-up 1941-1973*. Charlottesville, Va.: Hampton Roads Publishing, 2002.

Good, Timothy. *Above Top Secret: The Worldwide UFO Cover-up*. New York: William Morrow & Company, 1988.

Hall, David Michael. *UFOs: A Century of Sightings*. Lakeville, Minn.: Galde Press, 1999.

Marrs, Jim. *Alien Agenda: Investigating the Extraterrestrial Presence Among Us*. New York: HarperCollins Publishers, 1997.

UFO ORGANIZATIONS

The J. Allen Hynek Center for UFO Studies (CUFOS)
2457 West Peterson Avenue
Chicago, IL 60659
(773) 271-3611
Infocenter@cufos.org
http://www.cufos.org

CUFOS publishes *The International UFO Reporter* (*IUR*) four times a year. This organization is composed of civilians who are interested in solving the UFO mystery. The *IUR* contains scholarly articles by leading researchers on the latest developments in the field.

The Mutual UFO Network (MUFON)
P.O. Box 369
Morrison, CO 80465
(303) 932-7709
(800) 836-2166 (sighting hotline)
mufonhq@aol.com
http://www.mufon.com

MUFON is the world's largest civilian UFO research organization. Each month they publish *The MUFON UFO Journal*, which features recent sightings and research. They have chapters in each state, with each state having a section director who organizes investigations, trains new field investigators and sets up local meetings. If you are interested in becoming a MUFON field investigator, MUFON has a training manual and a take-home test. MUFON is always looking for new and young investigators to help record the thousands of cases that occur each year across the world.

The National UFO Reporting Center (NUFORC)
(206) 722-3000 (sighting hotline)
http://www.nuforc.org

The National UFO Reporting Center is the nation's largest collection center for UFO reports. Researcher Peter Davenport in Washington State heads the center. It receives dozens of cases each day. Volunteers then categorize and list the cases on the NUFORC Web site according to time, date, location, and type of encounter. Open to the public, NUFORC has proved itself a valuable tool in studying the UFO phenomenon. To date, NUFORC has catalogued more than 40,000 separate UFO cases.

UFO Newsclipping Service (UFONS)
#2 Caney Valley Drive
Plumerville, AR 72127-8725
The UFONS newsletter, edited by Lucius Farish, is a collection of
UFO newspaper articles published each month across the world,
and is a vital tool for researchers who want to keep updated con-
cerning current UFO activity.

WEB SITES

Black Vault
http://www.blackvault.com
Founded by researcher John Greenwalde Jr., this Web site focuses on
the alleged government cover-up of UFOs. Using the Freedom
of Information Act (FOIA), numerous researchers have obtained
official government documents that detail the United States Government's involvement with UFOs. This Web site contains many
of these official documents.

UFO Evidence
http://www.ufoevidence.org
This high-quality Web site brings together a wide variety of UFO
evidence and provides a good introduction to the phenomenon of
aliens and UFOs.

Bibliography

Barker, Gray. *They Knew Too Much About Flying Saucers.* New York: University Books, 1956.

Berlitz, Charles and William L. Moore. *The Roswell Incident.* New York: Berkley Books, 1988.

Billig, Otto. *Flying Saucers—Magic In the Skies.* Cambridge, Mass.: Shenkman Publishing Company, Inc., 1982.

Birnes, William J. *The UFO Magazine, UFO Encyclopedia.* New York: Simon & Schuster, 2004.

Blum, Ralph and Judy Blum. *Beyond Earth: Man's Contact With UFOs.* New York: Bantam Books, 1974.

Burt, Harold E. *Flying Saucers 101: Everything You Ever Wanted to Know About Unidentified Flying Objects.* Sunland, Calif.: UFO Magazine, Inc., 2000.

Chalker, Bill. *The Oz Files: The Australian UFO Story.* Potts Point, Australia: Duffy & Snellgrove, 1996.

Colombo, John Robert. *UFOs Over Canada.* Ontario, Canada: Hounslow Press, 1991.

Connelly, Dwight. *The World's Best UFO Cases.* Martinsville, Ill.: Bookseller, Inc., 2004.

Crystall, Ellen. *Silent Invasion: The Shocking Discoveries of a UFO Researcher.* New York: Paragon House, 1991.

Dolan, Richard M. *UFOs and The National Security State: Chronology of a Coverup, 1941–1973.* Charlottesville, Va.: Hampton Roads Publishing, 2002.

Druffel, Ann & D. Scott Rogo. *The Tujunga Canyon Contacts: Updated Edition.* New York: Signet Books, 1988.

Fawcett, Lawrence & Barry J. Greenwood. *Clear Intent: The Government Cover-up of the UFO Experience.* Englewood Cliffs, N.J.: Prentice-Hall, Inc., 1984.

Feschino Jr., Frank C. *The Braxton County Monster: The Cover-up of the Flatwoods Monster Revealed*. Charleston, W.Va.: Quarrier Press, 2004.

Flammonde, Paris. *UFO Exist*. New York: Ballantine Books, 1976.

Fowler, Raymond E. *Casebook of a UFO Investigator*. Englewood Cliffs, N.J.: Prentice-Hall, Inc., 1981.

Friedman, Stanton T. *Top Secret/Majic*. New York: Marlow & Company, 1996.

Fuller, John G. *Aliens in the Skies: The New Battle of the Scientists*. New York: Berkley Medallion Books, 1969.

———. *The Interrupted Journey*. New York: Berkley Medallion Books, 1966.

Good, Timothy. *Above Top Secret: The Worldwide UFO Cover-up*. New York: William Morrow & Company, Inc., 1988.

Hall, Michael David. *UFOs: A Century of Sightings*. Lakeville, Minn.: Galde Press, 1999.

Hesemann, Michael and Philip Mantle. *Beyond Roswell: The Alien Autopsy Film, Area 51 & The U.S. Government Coverup of UFOs*. New York: Marlowe & Company, 1997.

Hickson, Charles and William Mendez. *UFO Contact at Pascagoula*. Tucson, Ariz.: Wendelle C. Stevens, 1983.

Huneeus, Antonio. "UFO Hoaxes." *Fate Magazine* 47, no. 534 (September 1994): 36–41.

Hynek, J. Allen. *The UFO Experience: A Scientific Inquiry*. New York: Ballantine Books, 1987.

Jung, Carl G. *Flying Saucers: A Modern Myth of Things Seen in the Sky*. Princeton, N.J.: Bollingen Paperbacks, 1978.

Kitei, Lynn. *The Phoenix Lights*. Charlottesville, Va.: Hampton Roads, 2004.

Ledger, Don and Chris Styles. *Dark Object: The World's Only Government-Documented UFO Crash*. New York: Dell Publishing, 2001.

Lorenzen, Coral and Jim Lorenzen. *Abducted!: Confrontations With Beings From Outer Space*. New York: Berkley Medallion Books, 1966.

———. *Encounters with UFO Occupants*. New York: Berkley Publishing Corp., 1976.

Mantle, Philip and Paul Stonehill. *Mysterious Sky: Soviet UFO Phenomenon*. Baltimore, Md.: www.publishamerica.com., 2006.

Michel, Aime. *Flying Saucers and the Straight Line Mystery.* New York: Criterion Books, 1958.

Randle, Ph.D., Kevin D. *Invasion Washington: UFOs Over the Capitol.* New York: HarperCollins Publishers, 2001.

Randle, Kevin D. and Donald R. Schmitt. *The Truth About the UFO Crash At Roswell.* New York: M. Evans & Company, 1994.

The Roper Organization. *Unusual Personal Experiences: An Analysis of the Data from Three National Surveys.* Las Vegas, Nev.: Bigelow Holding Corporation, 1992.

Steiger, Brad. *Project Bluebook: The Top Secret UFO Findings Revealed.* New York: Ballantine Books, 1976.

Strieber, Whitley. *Communion: A True Story.* New York: William Morrow & Company, Inc., 1987.

Thompson, Richard. *Alien Identities.* San Diego, Calif.: Govardhan Hill Publishing, 1993.

Time-Life. *The UFO Phenomenon.* Alexandria, Va.: Time-Life Books, Inc, 1987.

Trench, Brinsley Le Poer. *The Flying Saucer Story.* New York: Ace Books, Inc., 1966.

Vallee, Jacques. *Anatomy of a Phenomenon: UFOs in Space.* New York: Ballantine Books, 1965.

———. *The Invisible College: What a Group of Scientists Has Discovered About UFO Influences on the Human Race.* New York: E.P. Dutton, 1975.

———. *Passport to Magonia: On UFOs, Folklore and Parallel Worlds.* Chicago, Ill.: Contemporary Books, 1969.

Walton, Travis. *The Walton Experience.* New York: Berkley Publishing Corp., 1978.

Warren, Larry and Peter Robbins. *Left At East Gate.* New York: Marlow and Company, 1997.

Wilkins, Harold T. *Flying Saucers On the Attack.* New York: Ace Books, 1954.

Wood, Ryan S. *Majic Eyes Only: Earth's Encounters with Extraterrestrial Technology.* Broomfield, Colo.: Wood Enterprises, 2005.

Index

About the Author

PRESTON DENNETT began investigating UFOs in 1986 when he discovered that his family, friends, and co-workers were having dramatic encounters. He is a field investigator for the Mutual UFO Network (MUFON) and a member of the Center for UFO Studies (CUFOS). He has investigated UFO encounters of virtually every type, and has been referred cases by the local police. He has written ten books and more than 100 articles, with translations into German, Portuguese, Chinese, and Icelandic. He has appeared on numerous television and radio programs. His research has been featured in leading magazines including *Fate*, the *MUFON Journal* and *UFO Magazine*, and in newspapers such as the *LA Times*, the *LA Daily News*, and the *Dallas Morning News*. He has taught classes about UFOs and lectures across the United States. He currently lives in Canoga Park, California. His Web site is http://www.prestondennett.com.

About the Consulting Editor

ROSEMARY ELLEN GUILEY is one of the foremost authorities on the paranormal. Psychic experiences in childhood led to her lifelong study and research of paranormal mysteries. A journalist by training, she has worked full time in the paranormal since 1983, as an author, presenter, and investigator. She has written 31 nonfiction books on paranormal topics, translated into 13 languages, and hundreds of articles. She has experienced many of the phenomena she has researched. She has appeared on numerous television, documentary, and radio shows. She is also a member of the League of Paranormal Gentlemen for Spooked Productions, a columnist for *TAPS Paramagazine*, a consulting editor for *FATE* magazine, and writer for the "Paranormal Insider" blog. Ms. Guiley's books include *The Encyclopedia of Angels*, *The Encyclopedia of Magic and Alchemy*, *The Encyclopedia of Saints*, *The Encyclopedia of Vampires, Werewolves, and Other Monsters*, and *The Encyclopedia of Witches and Witchcraft*, all from Facts On File. She lives in Maryland and her Web site is http://www.visionaryliving.com.